73

Oh God Get Out Get Out
Bill Moran

ငဒ

Write Bloody Publishing
America's Independent Press

Los Angeles, California

1ˢᵗ edition.
ISBN: 978-1938912-68-9

Interior Layout by Madison Mae Parker
Cover Designed by Brandon Lyon
Author Photo by Christopher Diaz
Proofread by Gary Lovely and Lino Anunciacion
Edited by Gary Lovely and Laura Mullen
Type set in Bergamo from www.theleagueofmoveabletype.com

Printed in Tennessee, USA

Write Bloody Publishing
Los Angeles, CA

Support Independent Presses
writebloody.com

To contact the author, send an email to writebloody@gmail.com

MADE IN THE USA

Oh God Get Out Get Out

For You
& I

(on the tile,
Dec 2015)

OH GOD GET OUT GET OUT

ACTIVATED CHARCOAL HEALING RITUAL

0.

ACTIVATED CHARCOAL: INDICATIONS:
POISONING AND OVERDOSE ACTIVATED
CHARCOAL IS GROUND INTO POWDER
MIXED INTO FLUID AND INGESTED   IT
WILL BIND TO TOXIN IN STOMACH AND
CARRY OUT OF BODY   YOUR GOAL
AS EMT IS TO REMOVE TOXIN FROM SYSTEM
ADMINISTER   MED   AND   TRANSPORT
REPORT NAME DOSE ROUTE TIME CHANGE
IN MENTAL STATUS ETC   REASSESS
INTERVENTIONS EVERY 5 MIN   DOCUMENT
IT ALL

0.

PROCEDURE: ADMINISTER PER ORAL
IT IS OFTEN PREMIXED WITH LAXATIVE
SORBITOL AS POISONS MAY BREAK FREE
INTO BLOODSTREAM IF ALLOWED TO SIT
IN BODY THRU A NORMAL DAY   IT IS A
SUSPENSION KEEP SHAKING CONTAINER
TO KEEP CHARCOAL FROM SEPARATING
AND SETTLING AT BOTTOM DARK FLUID
LOOKS INKY AND UNAPPETIZING TO MOST
DELIVER IN OPAQUE STYROFOAM CUP
WITH   LID   AND   STRAW   TO   HIDE
APPEARANCE   SORBITOL SWEETENS
THE TASTE BUT MOST WILL VOMIT AND
WONT   BE   ABLE   TO   FINISH
ENCOURAGE THEM   EXPLAIN   THEY
HAVE TO START OVER IF THEY CANNOT
INGEST IT ALL   MUST HAVE ENTIRE 50
GRAM DOSE FOR IT TO   REMOVE ALL
POISON   KEEP   SHAKING   IF
PATIENT NEEDS A   BREAK EXPLAIN   IT
IS OK BUT AGAIN   YOU HAVE TO
HAVE IT ALL OR   GO THROUGH IT ALL
OVER AGAIN   OK TRY HARD NOT TO
GIVE UP OR VOMIT AGAIN OK   OK HERE
YOU GO:

1.
i'm a kid and i'm holding onto my entry ticket and
i hate this haunted house so i

ask the dead
guy on the table am i

allowed to
leave he says

what oh sorry
you've already gone too

far the only exit
is at the end and then i

get old i'm in an ambulance
explaining to this nervous kid

you're going to hate it but
you have to have it all ok ok here you go:

O.

[nervous]   Um,   hi,   welcome
to the Chris Farley show.   I'm–Chris   Farley.   And,
my guest tonight is–   one   of   the–   greatest
musicians–   or, rock musicians   ever

[hits himself]   *GOD THAT SOUNDED STUPID.*
God, I–   idiot. I never know how to en– start these things.

–Chris Farley
(as Chris Farley

BILDUNGSROMAN ((A GUIDED TOUR

0.
Usually, it goes like:

Boy wakes up in   wall,
has to eat his way   out.

(Boy goes all day vomiting plaster into the shower (or dad's loafers, hopes he falls down the drain.

(How far our Featherweight champ does lean on the ropes of his grief ring.

(How rudely he appears from the wall like a hickey, head-sized & foul-mouthed (and I bet that's what he is: a loud bruise (you have to be, when your family history is such a 100-year fist.

(It's Halloween in July and I bet you're wondering 'what's with the plastic vampire teeth, honey?'   (It's practice.

(Boy been reading up on blueprints, 'load bearing', Jonah, anatomy of whales. Woke up in daddy's briefcase one morning, in daddy's gun closet the next, then in daddy himself   (That's three whales in three days   (C h e w e d clean through all three.

(Boy wakes up in kitchen wall, has to eat his way out.
(Boy wakes in bottle of Vicodin, has to eat his way out.
(Boy Hero, in epic quest, crosses physical threshold which reveals new landscape of psychological and spiritual maturity (but sometimes he gets stuck (in between and just boils there with his showerbeer.
(Worried Boy wakes up in himself, has to white pill his way out.
(Boy wakes in a Robin Williams hive with honey teeth, laughing or choking or both.
(Kitchen is Chris Farley's giant mouth. The garage, Shane MacGowan's. You can rearrange things, sure, but this house won't howl any less loud.
(Boy wakes with 100 faces, none the one he started out with.
(Boy wakes behind the holy eyelids of his parish priest and Lord, 100 showers wouldn't be enough.
(Boy wakes up in his Want, has to want his way out.
(Boy draws a bath of hormone and dozes off in the tub. Dreams he's JFK. Marilyn explodes out the showerhead singing Happy Birthday straight at his

head.
(Boy dreams of icing on her $12,000 dress. Of men in nice suits doing things so
vile, it rots the shower curtain right off the rod.
(Boy sees two options here: be dead Kennedy or Dead Kennedy. In his sleep
he sings 'California Über Alles'.
(Boy wakes in daddy's cologne, has to apologize it off his arms.
(Brother wakes up inside his sister's cast. She opens it with a cake knife and asks
him to leave.
(Boy wakes up chewing 'sorry', loud as a wedding bell.
(Boy wakes in the wedding cake of his Anxiety, has to sweet talk his way out.
((Boy wakes in his Anxiety again, this time with lockjaw. He stays in there all
day.
(((Boy imagines front teeth sinking into icing, his oh so nervous icing.
((((Boy wakes in an oven and rolls into an oven and this is his life.
(((((Boy wakes in bed, bloated, hungry. Gives up. Thinks it's probably rain
knocking on his window but who knows, could be teeth.
((((((Boy is actually 100 boys and all their teeth are fake. Grins fulla glass or pills
but goddamn, the kids look sharp.
(((((((Boy oh boy, what a quiet kid. What a strong jaw.

((((((((
Ok, usually it goes like:
Boy wakes up in the kitchen

wall, just behind the refrigerator.
Ok so he's inside the kitchen wall,

and at the same time, somehow,
he's also standing in the kitchen.

Ok, ok usually
Boy wheels the fridge

            out of his own way, and waits
            for his new, happy, whole self to

            emerge from behind it.
            But today, instead,

            he just pours a glass of white wine
            and leaves it there

I'M WALKING THROUGH A HAUNTED HOUSE IN LOUISIANA AND WON'T KEEP MY BIG MOUTH SHUT

0.

'cause i saw something five years ago and now i'm a deathexpert or whatever so i pull the actor aside mid-scene and give him notes: ok so that arterial bleed looks great, real scary: but i've seen this before and your version looks too uhhh right: if you're going for realism, scene's gotta look off, hasty: like you wouldn't hold onto the gun: you're too surprised ya know it was louder than you thought: leave it on the floor like ten feet back 'cause you tripped: also, it doesn't take the whole head off: three quarters, sure, but leave a cheek: offer it up for a kiss like Kim Novak ya know in *Vertigo?*: ok ass up to god: the dead aren't easily embarrassed but they would be: lose the plain white tee: this has to be american: yeah a football jersey but not a local team: humans aren't that simple and 'the saints' is too overt or: fuck what i said and kill yourself different yeah get off the couch moonlight as a medic see some shit bottle it up casually abuse alcohol and disappoint your family for ohh five years and then let it all out at once and don't stop talking: yeah that would be really real: huh? i'm holding up the line? oh you're trying to make a living? who the hell am i? well i used to be a medic now i'm One Long Howl thanks for asking: hey christ dude i'm trying to help: na you go to hell: haha fuck off i'm not going anywhere: hey you don't scare me dead guy: yeah yeah you can't touch me it's the law asshole: i don't give a shit man i don't signify shit man i got no words and i won't shut up: i am the Great Big Mouth and oh my god i howl for ever and ever hahahahaha: and then i go home and listen to Deathmetal and drink till i black out and talk in my sleep if anything to keep my mouth busy: if i don't use it i'm not alive: i'm scared i'm tired i wanna die i don't wanna die: some nights i turn my headlights off on country roads or: i write this shitty poem all

9

over again and don't know how to end it or: i turn
my house lights off and run from room to room
to room in pitch black and don't slow down or:

GIVE UP YEAH GO AWAY

(40 teenage faces   (a burning bush (that the
Deathmetal god talks through   (and he says giveup
giveup there is no god   (big   enough. you   can
wear this instead:

(here wear 'give' and 'up' like earrings and die
young in your sunday best. you can yell giveup like a
bullet hanging in hot Houston air like a Xanax angel
looking away from heaven and down at us, as if you
called his name,   as if you called your own:

(ok 'giveup' isn't god's real name but hell it's a lot closer
than 'god'   ('giveup' eight and a half times
is closer

(or you can hurl   a bullet or   b u t t e r f l y
knife or pill or 40 or black metal record or vomit up
in the air above you it's up   to you   these are all
ok ways to say   'god'

(   ) giveup is a new moon in a dirty sky   an old dog
open-mouthed for your best howl you   can
go into the night like an At The Gates shirt you   can
wear all black like a giveup bath you   can
give up yeah be a ghost with us

0.
you can set your clothes on fire and then wear them

0.
you can listen to Deathmetal music

0.
it's ok   you have

0.
options

DREAM FUNERAL

0.
It's not black, but grandma's Cadillac is still an ok
hearse. Roll up to the nicest church then keep going.
To the daiquiri place. Get whatever you want.

Let me go to glory in a bowling alley, Lord. Let it
look like how I lived: all aesthetic. Champagne veneer.
Walls like coffee breath, please. Have to yell my
eulogy over the vacuum cleaner. Wheel me out to
the center lane, right about here that's good. Ok go
ahead, don't be nice:

0.
'Ben always wanted to go away then he went away
good for him.'

(I hope everyone gets my name wrong

'After Benny Boy went oh-for-one in CPR, kissing
scared the hell out of him.'

(Amen

'Had a mouth fulla lemons. He'd say sorry, last time I
touched lips like this, I failed and one of us died.'

(Good. Really pile it on

'Whose wedding is this?'

(Everyone's

0.
Believers, rise and crack your knuckles with the
Xanax choir. Pour forties down every lane and gutter.
Gloss over half my shitty life. Kiss my middle fingers.
Call my exes. Have them stick their gum under my
eight-hundred dollar casket. Stuff wet towels in all the
brass horns. Swear to god, if I hear one trombone
start up with 'Amazing Grace' I'll haunt that shit
straight to the pawn shop (second line if you really
want to, but don't make believe it's for me. Ok I'm
gonna need a winedrunk Anyone to turn the wine
into wine, please. Gonna need them to drop

their cake in the casket, fake cry, and fish it out. Yeah. Grieve like that.

0.

The angels of death have flown in from Los Angeles wearing Charlie Chaplin's makeup. Holy barbers come to cut my hair and hollow me out. Jokes on them (This casket's been empty. I'm not going to a better place. Wasn't here to begin with.

Ok everyone watch me get this haircut. High and tight, '55, Los Feliz, all pomp all fade all nostalgia no heart. No heart. Nothing in here but a can of pomade. I open my chest and hold it in the air. And the L.A.ngels of death sing, 'O there you are, baby. Almost didn't recognize our kin.'

0.

I know: 'But *arrangements* must be made. What would you like when you die?'   Glad you asked:

I'd like you to arrange your weepy faces away from me amen.
I'd like Napalm Death on the intercom amen.
I hope it blows the speakers to shit amen.
Hope the velvet curtains catch fire amen.
Hope you save the cake and leave the glitzy casket inside amen.
Hope it tips and you get a good look at my bleached teeth smiling. Ugly but true. Like too many white blood cells and what they do. Like this expiration date on our heads. Like what you'd like to forget (but I won't let you. Amen.

No. I'm dead now. I don't have try so hard to be nice. Or liked. Least of all to myself. By myself. It doesn't matter. Only half the songs I loved turned out true: the ones too loud to hear the words. Pope says 'no marriage in heaven' and I say 'good.' I am now how I've always felt:

on the way

out:

with an Irish
goodbye:

0.
dying
is so mean.

it's a mean thing to do. and i want
to be a nice man, i do.

i want to mean something good.
i don't want to grow old

and mean and leave
you nice people

(and good news: i don't have to
if i'm already alone

(alright. you want my will,
you got it:

leave me here and don't wait up
leave me here and don't wait up
leave me and don't wait don't leave
leave me and wait don't leave me
leave me and wait don't leave me
leave and wait don't leave
leave wait don't leave
leave don't leave
leave don't leave

don't leave
don't leave

don't
don't

don't

O.

All we love we leave behind.

—Converge

How could you go without me?

—Oathbreaker

ACTIVATED BAD NEWS HEALING RITUAL

0.

ADMINISTER PER ORAL   POISONS MAY
BREAK FREE IF ALLOWED TO SIT IN BODY
FLUID   IS   INKY   MESSY   UNAPPETIZING
MANY WILL VOMIT AND   QUIT   EARLY
KEEP SHAKING IF PATIENT NEEDS A BREAK
ENCOURAGE THEM   EXPLAIN YOU
HAVE TO HAVE IT ALL AND   HOLD IT
DOWN OR START ALL OVER   AGAIN
EXPLAIN EXPLAIN OK AGAIN   EXPLAIN:

0.

INFORMING   FAMILY   AND   FRIENDS:
IMPORTANT: DO NOT USE EUPHEMISMS
DO NOT SUGARCOAT   DO NOT GIVE ANY
APPEARANCE OF FALSE HOPE   STUDIES
SHOW   YOUR   WORDS   ARE   KEY   TO
GRIEVING   PROCESS   HALFWAY
ACKNOWLEDGE IT NOW   AND THEY WILL
HALFWAY ACCEPT IT LATER   THEY WILL
REFER   BACK   TO   YOUR   WORDS   AND
REHASH THEM AND REFUSE TO ACCEPT
THE STORY   'WE LOST HIM': WE CAN'T
FIND HIM BUT HE'S HERE   'HE'S GONE':
TO THE BEACH FOR VACATION BUT WILL BE
BACK   'WE COULDN'T SAVE HIM': BUT
HE CAN BE SAVED   OK DELIVER EACH
WORD LIKE AN ARM TO GRAPPLE WITH
CUT   THE FAT   GIVE THEM
EIGHT   STRONG   FACTS:

0.

PROCEDURE: INHALE   LOOK THEM IN
THE EYE   THEIR FACE: SILVER TROUT
THE NEWS: OCTOPUS ARMS   INHALE
WATER   SPIT INK INTO THEIR
MOUTH   AND   ALL   AROUND
DARK FLUID   INKY   UNAPPETIZING
IF IT SOUNDS HARSH OR UNSYMPATHETIC
IT'S   BECAUSE   THE   NEWS   IS

BOTH   LOVE THIS STRANGER
ENOUGH TO   LET THEM KNOW WHAT
THEY HAVE TO   GO   THROUGH
STARTING NOW   (IF THEY HATE YOU
YOU DID IT RIGHT   PRACTICE IN   THE
AMBULANCE   MOUTH   THE WORDS (
LIKE A TROUT   (IN THE BELLY OF A BOAT
OPEN   YOUR LIPS   USE   YOUR
DIAPHRAGM   REHEARSE YOUR   LINES
THEN GO OUT   THERE AND   D E L I V E R
THEM TWICE   REWORD TO REINFORCE
AND LEAVE   NO ROOM FOR QUESTION
NO EUPHEMISMS   NO SUGARCOATING
OK CADET TURN TO YOUR PARTNER AND
HUG THEM   TO YOUR BEAK   DON'T
LOOK AWAY   AT   THAT HOLY ARM
AROUND YOUR OWN BELLY   HOLDING
YOU   UP AND UP   TO HEAVEN'S WIDE
MOUTH   OK REPEAT   LIKE WE RE
HEARSED: *YOUR   FRIEND   HAS*
DIED.   *YOUR   FRIEND   IS*
DEAD.

0.
OK GOOD AGAIN:

OSR

0.
'Dandelion',
from the French for

'the lion's tooth'
but we already know this (how bones break:

easy.

1.
Ok first the bull, then Bourbon Street. Come morning
we'll be gone. But first we have to bury this goddamn bull.

Your pop's most expensive steer, Christopher, died of a virus. Alright
so we did what we had to do: bought rope and beer, hitched him to
your truck by his hind legs, and toasted a six-pack each to some dead
animal. At dawn we'll drag his body out to the clearing where the grass is green
and the dandelions are bone:

Easy. If you've ever eaten painkillers without counting them first, you can bury
a bull. It's the same thing (you leave it in the grass and let it

sink. Dragging it out

there is harder. Like last time, a nice march: a mardi gras of cattle: cows and calves
second-lining behind your Ford: brass hides and horns polished to a sheen: tuba
and trombone heads hung and blaring off-key for Christopher,

as if cattle could wail, right? As if 'funeral' is something that happens to us, easy
as 'laugh' or 'yawn'. As if 'Bye & Bye' could parade-float up out a calf's belly. As
if grief were milk.

The grass was the jaw of a tuba. We untied the bull, left him there, and headed
for the Big

Easy.

1.

On Bourbon Street you have hand-grenade belly, your belt tied around your forehead like it's holding you together, slack end hanging, a horn of faux leather, aimed angry at the earth, when you get the news:

'your brother's dead'

(You loose the belt. Your head falls clean
off the bone.

0.

In Texas, I help you tie your heart to your truck's hitch and we follow your little brother's hearse to the cemetery, smearing your heart on Old San Antonio Road like sick livestock 'til it's either a handful of dandelions or

bones (I don't know.
I take a bite and I find
out (And again I dream that

I am the grass. Grief
grows up
from my belly. Little bulls
walk on my grief field, grazing.
Again the bulls wail:
'Let go

or be dragged. Let
go or be

dragged'
Again

0.

and again, we've watched kids eaten into East Texas grass and now it's sunk in: that god is bone. Indeed we have dragged our god so far, all that's left is the bone. Even that's chipping off. We call it
'dandelion'
or 'depression'
or I don't know, anything
that will

grow back.

(One day, Bourbon street will go white with dandelions and we will go there to die. We who lead our hearts to the Bull's Teeth by the hand. We who graze on your brother's name: our breakfast of grass. And eat his cufflinks, his boutonniere, the white flowers right out of his hands.

(Our wax eyes we do not close. We know how easy the wax does melt. We know it is not milk. It is hot. Yet I lap it off your cheek anyway and bar hop to the Minotaur's front door and black out. Our Grief is a red cape. Us bulls, we dance like this and call it Whygod.

(Grief is the virus
(The medicine is More

(It's too goddamn hot to bury
a kid today but we do it

       0.
       (Hitch up your heart, your Sunday best, your father by
       his leg, and drive. Friend, this is the tax we are to pay
       and we   pay it

       (Us bulls don't know how to die (yeah but we
       do it anyway. We do what we have to do:

       (hand in our coins   (and brothers   (keep a
       straight face   (act sober

       0.
       (A very thirsty Heaven begs us to sink into it (but in
       Texas, there's always another bull or boy to bury first:

KING CAKE

0.

In the Beginning, God built the firmament of Heaven
and declared, 'I am exhausted, O
I am lonely' and then hurled himself off
its edge. He crashed in Houston (3900 Yupon)
and cracked into a hundred pieces and
became all of

Us.
A God of a Hundred Different Things. Amen.

1.

O Lord, I've read Dante: a couple sad writers walk
into Hell and talk to a hundred dead friends: a forest
of Acacias. Inside every tree: another kid who has
killed himself and pawned his body for wine and
anxiety meds. A hundred boys recorked into thorn

trunks   (Yeah well this spine also creaks like a
two-by-four   ('I too have been close to it'   (in that
dark wood.

(Gracious God, yesterday I woke up hungover, got dressed
up, and buried
my best friend,
because I had to.

(Michael dove from a nine-story garage (from a nine-
story woods (from his own head because of the heat
and howling,
because he had to.

(God I hope you gave him room in there.

(God of Untucked Shirts, I am here to buy his body
back from you. I cannot afford it.

(O Houston God, I've come to your house with king
cake in a ziploc bag (like he and I used to (a couple

kids eating cake in Mass, with our bare hands. It tasted
more like your body than the bread they had there.

(O God of Diving and Diving Boards and Dead
Comedians, God of Chris Farley, of His Gold
Frosting Laugh and Orange Pill Bottle (Hail Chris,
holy King with bark inside his lip and belly of sap,
you   laugh.
I catch it and hold it like an ax handle. Hail,
Chris, pray for us. We who built blanket forts
and laughed until we threw up in them. We who eat
laughter and Xanax until we throw up and die.
(Blanket God of Blanket Forts that won't hold
up (like we won't   (after Mikey's funeral, I broke

(into a bar. I hung sheets on the taps and barstools
like   crappy   Church   beams.   Like
I was in your gilded teeth, Lord. I poured
a couple pints and laid in there, dressed to the
nines, Inferno in hand, and I asked you:

(God With Icing On His Fingers, God Who Holds
Us, why are you eating us alive like cake? Are you
asleep? Have you been sleeping through this? (God
Who I Want To Hate But Don't, God I Don't
Understand, God of Dead Best Friends, I'm coming
up there. I'm going to knock on Heaven. And when
you open up, I'm going to hit you square in the chin.
It'll ring like two glasses toasting. And I'll hold my
aching fist like a book's spine and quote
Romans at you   ('What a wretched man
I am,   who will save me from this Body of Death?'

(O God of Open Bars, I clean up good. I've been a
groomsman and pallbearer in one week. Even caught
the garter   (and I wish I could've caught you like that:

0.

(a garter
(right out of Houston's hot sky.

(I left it on the dance floor with my slice of cake. I
said   (I can't swallow this (I don't want it. I am done
with Dante and his dumb Inferno. It became too hot
to hold so I ate it (I chewed every page, tried to talk to
my dead friend again   (it didn't work

(But Dante came back up, from the hell in
my belly, in my friend's voice:

('What do you gain from shielding in me?
Why grieve in places where you hurt?
Why feed on the foliage?'

What if the medicine's worse than the illness?
Why go to Hell and back, like this famous writer.
Why go through it all again?

(And I quote him
back to him:

                              'Because of the love I bear my native
                              Florence, because of the love I bear
                                   love because of love I bear

                                        'love because of love of
                                                  I bear I
                                                    bear

('I gather up the scattered leaves, and give them
back to the suicide'   like a wedding invite, like medicine:

(You   are   not   the   last   thing   you   did   amen
(You   were   sick   and   now   you're   not   amen
(Heaven's gate is Houston cement. You went clean through amen
(I heard God ring you on asphalt like glasses clinking amen
God's   not   grass   or   concrete,   he's   king   cake,   and   you
cannonballed   into   Him.   His   gold   icing   went   everywhere:

(amen   (amen
(It looks   great, buddy.
You clean
up good.

O.

[Nervous]   Ok– ok–   you   remember,
when, you were with the Beatles? And–   you
were supposed to be dead? ...And uh, everyone
thought that you were dead, or somethi–
and   ...   Uh, that was–   um–   a hoax,
right?

–Chris Farley
(as Chris Farley

ACTIVATED CHARCOAL HEALING RITUAL

0.

AGAIN: YOUR GOAL AS EMT IS TO REMOVE
ALL POISON FROM SYSTEM   DARK FLUID
IS INKY UNAPPETIZING   DELIVER IN
APPROPRIATE   CONTAINER   KEEP
SHAKING CONTAINER TO KEEP CHARCOAL
FROM SEPARATING AND SETTLING AT
BOTTOM   STATE AND RESTATE
DIFFERENTLY TO REINFORCE   AGAIN NO
EUPHEMISMS:

1.

Oh God Get Out Get Out   or Because I'm a
Hack and Can't Settle on One Title   or I Hate It
God I'll Have Another   or I Hate This God
I'll Have It All   or Holy Black Healing Water
or Hangover Cures   or Let This Cup Pass   or
Give Up Yeah Go Away   or   Ipecac   Happy
Hour   or Eucharist Buffet   or Eat
Your Way Out   or   Cake   &   Corpse
Paint   or Trve Norwegian Black Metal   or
Frøstbitten Black Metal Memes   or
All You Can Eat Anxiety or How To Bite A Halo In
Half   or   Holy   Schnikes
or Ghost Grits   or   Irish   Goodbye
or Eyes Open Eyes Open   or What If
The Medicine's Worse Than the Illness   or
I'm So Scared It Is   or I'm Scared This Won't
Actually Help Anyone   or It's a Lot to Swallow   or
It's All A Whole Lot   or You Have To Have It All
Ok   or   Ok   Good   Again:

ACTIVATED BAD MATH HEALING RITUAL

0.
Your friend is dead   Your friend has died

0.
I'm so sorry- yes- yes sir-   your friend is now-

0.
Yes   um, yes I am sorry (dead weight   weighs a
ton   (the tongue is the strongest muscle you have
(yes you have   heavy lifting to do: Your friend
died. Died is your friend is. Is your friend dead yes
(ok breathe underwater it's easy:

0.
Died is your died died.   Uh, dead your dead.
Your friend is your is dead.   Died the die. I'm so
sorry your   died the die. Yes he did die the die
yes (ok evaporate it's easy:

0.
Yes I'm so sorry   (I don't wanna hurt you. Don't
wanna say it: sad thing sad thing. No. I wanna
evaporate right fucking here. Wanna die the die
O God the word eatin' me up feet up 'til I'm only
my teeth, repeating what I dunno know how to say:

0.
Yes sir I am so sorry, your   is dead. Your   has
died.   Hi here your you   have to carry this yes   Hi
so sorry, you have to carry   this   sorry   Hi you can
evaporate now   Hi yes I has a sorry sorry.
Sorry.   I has a dead sorry. Sorry has a dead I. Sorry
is a dead yes. Yes I died sorry   Sorry, I
not saying this right.   It's hard to say this thing.
Sad thing.   Sorry, it's an odd time signature. All
math really.   Ok here   listen   to   Deathmetal
(death black doom sludge hardcore punk blah blah
(all Deathmetal   (It says   the death
better: organized: 0,
0, a couple 1's but mostly 0's out its mouth like a

waterfall   of sorry   ink   a guitar tab
ok lean into it   ok evaporate   into   math:

0.

'Dying Will Be The Death Of Me'   'Death   of   a
Dead Day'   'The Art of Dying'   'The   Frantic
Pace of Dying'   'Dead and Dripping'   'Into the Dead
Sky'   'Serenity Painted Death'   'Breeding Death'
'Death Cult Armageddon' (ok   you   get   the   idea.
Sorry your best friend is yeah ok you get it   (but hey I
ran the numbers,   I did the math and good
news: it's only math.   You   can   work
through this.   You can fill the sink with zeros and
dunk your head and keep it there all day   you
can breathe underwater if you just drown first   Ok
evaporate   Ok listen to Deathmetal   Ok
lean into this noise:

0.

(because your sister's on the phone telling you your
best friend passed away he's gone I mean I can give
you the numbers I can run them again but ok yeah,
see there was an accident he did accident he
accidented it doesn't add up but yeah he's gone
yeah ok but where'd he go hey where'd you go go
g0d   you g0d   where you g0 g0d   g0   g   0
000   000   001   0   :
00   10   1

0.
00 0   1
00 0

0.
0

0.

0.
Ok good again:

(*medcom medic 10?*   10, yes ma'am   *medcom*
you cleared the ER yet?   1 0 d o t t i n g
t's and crossing i's as we speak   *get*
going. i got a code for you. big one   g   o
ahead   *toning you now.*   [100 W AVE
K. GSW. P1] *medcom medic 10 alert: nolanville*
texas.   one zero zero west avenue k. gunshot wound.
priority one   10   medcom   received   and   en
route   to   one   zero   zero   west   avenue   k   nolanville
for   a   gunshot   wound.   goin'   lights   and   sigh-
reens   *okey doke 10 i have you en route at*
one forty-one A.M. for a gunshot wound to the head.
nolanville FD and PD on their way, UHF channel
100. be advised scene is not code four. again, we're not code
four yet. get all that?   1 0   m e d c o m
received. where we stagin'?   *good   question 10.*
ummm how 'bout i drop you at the methodist church on
3rd and Avenue--   medic 10 medcom i didn't
get   that   cross   street.   please   repeat   traffic
medcom 10 please stage at united methodist church on
3rd and Avenue I   10   received   staging   at
3rd and Avenue ay dios mio   [U H F:
Nolanville   PD   here.   come   on   in   y'all,
everything's   settled   here.   hope   you   like   haunted
houses]   *medcom 10 we have a code four. don't bother*
with the church. reroute to one zero zero west avenue k.
patient's in the backyard   1   0
received en   route   to   one   zero   zero   west   avenue
k   [UHF: Nolanville   FD   requesting   JP   at   one
zero zero w avenue k]   10 medcom, rumor is
JP's on his way   *not till i say he is, 10. i don't*
want to see that truck doin' under 100   h a h a
received   ...   *medcom medic 10*   y e s
medcom?   *aaaaand you can reduce to non-emergent*
travel   thanks love   *medcom medic 10, stick to*
radio traffic protocol   medic   10   medcom
received. over   *10,   no   one   says   'over'*
...   medic   10   medcom,   on   scene.
over   *alright, 10. i have you on sc-- at fift-*
--one——m   medcom   you're   fuzzy.   repeat

traffic   *-com---10 ---on scene---one--- a---*   ok
medcom the poet's head is a repeater tower   *i*
don't under-- and   ok   10   medcom   10   is
underground,   switching   to   Divine
Comedy   *receiv-- 10 I have you underg-- switching*
to Div--e Com--   ok   medcom,   you're   still
fuzzy. switching to UHF   *re---ved*   *be*
adv-   medic 10 medcom, ok switching to the
book of samuel   *received. be advised that*
none touch the young man absalom   10   medcom
patient contact. priority three. o   my   son
absalom *received. field medic 10 patient contact*
at samuel one fifty nine. priority--- ree   10 would
god i had died for thee   *received*   *davi--*
received 10   Godcom   be   advised   i   am   joab
kneeling at my fields   *field medic 10 repeat*
traffi--   i said his head is upturned earth.
the lord hath set my fields on fire   *i don't--*
he-- 10 repeat traf--   received lord, lord god
please don't set my fields on fire   *10 are you ab*
or davi-- or medic 10-- or dante 10--   received
Virgil   *--u don't make sen-- i'll need you*
to be lazar-   received. o lord o medcom my
mouth is so little *received 10 ok lose the names.*
stick to numbers, letters. it--- biggest language we got
an-- it--protocol   received   *r e c e i v e d*
received   *receive--*   r e c i e v e--
r e—   *-ved*   —
-

.

BOWIE KNIFE

(
sun
sun
sun
sun
sun
sun
sun
sun text
sun texas
sun texas is
sun texas is the
sun texas is the
son texas is the rea
son texas is the rea
son texas is the rea
son texas is the rea
son texas is the rea
son texas is the rea
son texas is the rea
son texas is the rea

son that the president's dead and all the good boys kill themselves before they become good men ain't no good men in texas only men with dull Knives men who file down their teeth who trepan the sun with a boy Knife who all want a jackie O to catch our roseheads like a vase only boys who are Knives only sonless fathers howling: i miss you Christopher my handsome

son
son
son
son

GODSALT

1.
salt

i'm Salt. sorry.   i'm b- Salt.   i'm bil- Salt. ok,
i'm pelican bill. i'm dinner bill.   i'm, i'm a comic
book called b- no Salt.   no,   i'm a comic called
Robin Salt Salt Williams.   i'm reading a comic called
sui- Salt and it's full of my friends dissolving. salty-
sorry-   let me salt-   start-
over:

1.
i'm driving to Galveston with my saltsalt friends
again. we are going to our favorite diner by the
beachsalt and everyone's still alivesalt. no one has
dissolved yet. it's salt ok. salty- sorry- i- i mean to
say 'sodium chloride' but say 'sodium cyanide' (it's an
easy mistake (all my friends drink the wrong one
accidentally on purpose (all my friends are turning
into salt in public pools, fountains, bathrooms,
sprinklers but never the ocean (they don't

dive into the anxietywater to die   (they already
swim in it (they just di-

ssolve (and so do i
(i'm
(i'm a lot of
i'm Lot and
everyone i love turns into
salt:

(why do they have to do that?
(why do they have to boil over onto my cheeks?
(how come crying feels a lot like cooking?
(how come it comes so easy in a public pool?
(how come everyone and no one sees me
(and i'm here and not here
(and how come i like it so much? dis-
(solving like you

(why'd you'd have to die and not come back
to our diner with me?
(i'm running out
of friends to have 3 a.m. eggs with
(i'm spill–
(ing

0.
salty– sorry–
ahhh salt. salt.
(i'm, i'm not mysalt
right now. ok
i'm trying to
salt it together
(i sob my selfsalt into salt (and salt (and salt (and salt (and
sink into the boiling water of this page and come up

      (
      here:

      i'm in Galveston, Texas.
      i'm dreaming
      of its chemical plants,
      ten minutes before dawn.
      i'm on the beach
      where all the trash of the gulf washes up:
      all the factory lights and white bags
      like glow worms in a cave, like spilt sal–
      stars

      (i name the pelicans after my dead friends.
      they dive down and scoop me into their bills
      (like a spoon (of salt

      (i don't know if i'm being carried or eaten
      (i don't know if i'm the Atlantic or the trash in it

      (i am a comic book called the Gulf of Mexico. ok, in
      this comic, old women draw circles of salt around
      graves like white lace (it keeps our loved ones from
      wandering off when they rise again   (it keeps them
      from leaving again   (it   keeps   my   grieving

in one place

(i'm writing a comic book called
You and you
stand up from the page and
wave
(good thing
i i wrote this in
salt salt

(i can't say my name but i can spell it in salt.
the word 'I' is a beach of salt.
the Gulf's white foam really is a salt veil
(it has the same salinity as my blood
(it keeps my dead friend
inside me
(it keeps me
inside me
with him
thank god

(i'm reading a comic book called You and it ends too
early   (all these words   wash   up   and   cover   us: i'm
salty-   sorry-   salty-   salty-   i'm   so   so
sorry   i'm so   salty   (i'm book of Isaiah say salt say:

'He will swallow up Death for all time.
and the salt salt godsalt will wipe
tearssalt from all

salt

salt

faces

salt

salt

(sorry

O.

Orangutans need to develop the fruit stare because ... the fruit is often hidden in the canopy of leaves. The fruit stare is an expression of reverie ... 'like thinking with your eyes' ... That's why they are so spaced-out.

—Vicki Hearne

Our eyes are open.

—Cult Leader

ACTIVATED COFFEE HEALING RITUAL

0.

YOUR GOAL IS TO REMOVE ALL THE
POISON   AGAIN AVOID SUGARCOATING

0.

i like my coffee like i like my metal: black and in the
morning and too much. no sugar no cream at the
station. the burnouts take it black and hey i also hate
myself ok so i'll drink smoke too (it's called method
acting (it's my first twenty-four and i'm green as hell
and about to go through hell so i drink hell and hope
i'll understand why: they do too   why:
expose yourself to all this   dark. why: take it in
black, holy: activated charcoal in white styrofoam,
'Oceanic' on vinyl, these pupils like empty   cups,
the water i wade in my dreams, all these words under
me: a yawning mouth: looking back up at
me i   look into this paper and see shitty
coffee i   look into that and see my young dumb
face i   look into myself and see oatmeal stout
for breakfast and i look   into   that   and   see
Hungover God hunched over this cup and i   look
into that and see me backstroking in his hangover
cure and i   look into that and see him yawning in
my face and i   look into that and see a cup of black holy
water and i   look into that and see my dead friends
and patients sitting at the bottom and they're looking
up at me and i am so   sorry i didn't
try harder and i   hold my nose and it tastes like hell
but i   drink it all uh huh i don't even stop to
breathe i   drink every last drop. i   lick the
bottom of the cup:

1.

i hate this place i'll have the usual
i hate this drink i'll have one more
i hate this drink i'll have one more
i hate the taste i'll have it all
i hate it god i'll have it all

EYES OPEN

( )
Another dead-you dream: another shadow puppet I have to type. Ok watch:
I shine my grieflight on the ceiling, hold this page in between, and lo and behold:
a pelican.

Alright watch me down this Thunderbird and I'll hit ya with a few trve fucking
black metal pelican facts: fact: to eat, the North American Brown Pelican
dives   into   the   sea   and   scoops   whole   fish   into   his   open
gullet.   He does this, every time, with his eyes open.   Watch:
eyes open   eyes open   eyes open   until the clap of water on his
cornea causes the bird to go blind. Watch: the trout below slowly go blurry,
dancing, mocking. Watch: everything go dark as the hungry bird, at last, starves
to death for his supper. Watch him: flying circles overhead: dumb halos:
writing giant zeroes: like it's his name: over the lake of his keyboard: eating only:
air   (these lights: are so bright: but i can still hear you: clapping:

(ok i'm having that dream again (i'm up   on stage and i think   (eyes open bill
this time keep your eyes open:

( )
the wind up here is nice and cool eyes open:
i like how it feels to fall eyes open:
and fast eyes open:
i am hungry eyes open:
for you eyes open:
or answers or anything but another bill eyes open:
full of dirty water eyes open:
god it tastes like medicine eyes open:
but i'll keep diving face first eyes open:
into the tv kitchen keyboard eyes open:
until i come up eyes open:
with you eyes open:
in my mouth eyes open:
or i drown eyes open:
oh god my eyes are wide open
(and i don't see you anywhere
(but i hear your ghost clapping (   )
crying:
i is 0 pen bill   (keep your i's open:

SIMIA DEI

1.

Look Bill, I know you're working twenty-fours and have expendable income now, but you can't get a banana tattoo on your hand. You'll have to look at it every day. Come on. It doesn't make sense.

(Hey what's with the bananas hung in your apartment? What do you mean 'human is the ape of god' and 'apes are the only real comedians?' You listening? Hey, look at me. Hey hey, look alive.

(How do you get so distracted at these funerals? You can look out to the trees all day, but I don't think your friend will reappear on one of its limbs. Go ahead and watch his favorite Farley films again and again (he won't drop out of the television.

(Wait what do you mean the Lord came back as an orangutan? What? We put him in a casino act? Huh?

(What do you mean the bananas hang inside you like ugly earrings, like question marks, and you're scared they're all rotten? What? How come bananas look like bones?

(Oh hold on. O god, is this about sex? Or kids or skeletons? How Houston keeps its kids in the refrigerator? How it peels them to the bone? Help I'm confused.

(Oh! Is it about how it eats us like fruit (bruised, hung, peeled, dried, chewed up? About the benjamins that grow on its branches? Oil-dipped bananas? Dying of hunger in a buffet? Eucharist binging? A canopy of leaves (but actually hate-church billboards? I've been watching you watch this shit and I think I get it. Wait, I don't get it.

(Ok let's see: I see Houston, right? And its chemical plants. Ok and what am I looking for? The lights? Hanging off the I I I-beams like electric leaves or holy fruit or angel sweat?

(Ohhhhh. O, I see. It's like, how a stranger can peel his own bruised head with a twelve gauge. How a young EMT can close his eyes and see chewed fruit for five fucking years. Yeah. It's like: you. In a bright yellow jacket. Helping a scared six-year old out the back of a totaled car. You wrap another yellow coat around him and look him in the eye and joke 'hey look, we're big ol' bananas'. You both laugh. The ambulance bites down. Yeah I think I get it.

(Shit, I don't get it. 100 questions and no answers. Huh? Who's peeling us wide? How come Heaven's yellow? It has jaundice? Houston has gout? This paper's a banana specked with blood? How's it so hard to swallow? Oh ok, it's like your abstract shit. Like: I think I kinda eat with my eyes. I think I look with my teeth. I wish I didn't have to talk about bananas to talk about dying. Wish I wasn't this hungry. Wish I didn't have to eat all this horrible shit: Houston covered in bananas foster, Galveston beach doused in sugar and fire, oil like burning rum, gospel and diabetic shock and OD's and PTSD and a leg cut open like old fruit and ok, ok hold on. I see a banana– hold on– I see a banana and a branch and a broken femur and oh it's kinda like: if I look at the limb long enough, I'll get it. I'll understand.

(Wait I don't get it. Hold on. Explain it slow. Ok it's like you're this orangutan– in fancy human clothes and anxious all the goddamn time– and you're buying a banana at the gas station. And the clerk explains 'if you survive that you'll survive anything haha' and then you walk out and kneel on the asphalt like it's a Houston shrine and ask Yellow God: peel open the clouds like leaves and appear, oh Hand of God if you're even here, yank my friend from his branch and hand him back to me' and Houston God says 'Huh?' with a full mouth and blank face and then keeps chewing on a banana. He eats it with a knife. Doesn't even look up.

(But hey, look. We're worried about you, ok? Yeah, I know, like you're this ape or whatever. And that's great. But you're hungry and your eyes are peeled on this page and you look like you've seen a ghost or your own obit in the Chronicle and you won't drop it with these bloody bananas and dead friends like one day they'll just reappear on the page like fucking magic. I mean, come on,   look at yourself: it doesn't make sense:

0.
ok whatever. i open   this keyboard like a
church and see blood but no   god i open   my
forearm and see   computer keys but   no   fruit i
open   this medicine bottle and alleluia:

bananas   ((far as the eye can see

(and I eat and eat and eat and   uh,   wait
(hold on   (hold on, i eat and, wait, i eat and, wait
(hold on   (uhhh hold on hold on, O wait, what?

    hold on:

BELLYLAUGH

1.
Boy watches himself on TV:

1.
Ok so a Bear trudges through Wisconsin snow in a dark woods. He happens upon an abandoned camp, and a kettle of hot stew that's been left boiling. He goes immediately to it, drinks, and burns his snout raw

(But, as Bears are wont to do, his instinctual defense is to lift the harmful thing up in his paws and hug it tight to his belly, as if to smother it to death. So he hugs the boiling kettle, searing his fur clean off

(Again, under attack, the Bear hugs the kettle even tighter and burns himself worse   (and   so   he hugs it tighter and hurts himself   (so   he hugs the kettle and hurts himself   (and   then Bear hugs kettle and Bear hugs kettle and bear hugs kettle bear hugs kettle bear hugs kettle and this idiot bear or

0   .
boy hugs kettle on live TV   and   the   applause
sounds like sloshing   and the cheers like
singeing fur and he learns well   (that laughter and
Powers are each a kind of warmth   (that   self-
harm is another way to eat   (that   his   body
is a hot kettle he cannot put down   (that   this
boiling sound is his first name   (and   the   big,
weepy animal learns how to wail   (kicking   like   a
toddler, through his own raw snout   (to   no   one
in particular:

MY HEROES WON'T DESCEND FROM HEAVEN AND HAUNT MY APARTMENT WITHOUT THE USUAL AMENITY REQUEST: LEMONADE

1.
40 lemons
400 lemon seeds
40 gallons of lemon juice
iodine
ipecac
everything

0.
everything

everything

everything you have
you have everything

everything you have everything
you have

everything you have in you
you have in you everything

everything you have in you everything
you have in you

everything you have left in you everything you have left in you everything you
have left everything

you have left everything

you have left everything
you have left

you have left everything
you have left

you left you
you left

left

you left
you

you
  u

  u
  u

  u
  .

I HATE THIS DRINK I'LL HAVE ANOTHER

0.

you are high-end pomade, my
Farley is here with clippers to cut

griefhair high and tight (Chris
you out but i won't let

him (10 couplets
on my ceiling (i catch my friends

10 inches (i write a net
souls like trout (i

watch them gleam
on TV (i watch

and gasp (like Chris
our favorite Farley flick (i mouth

the words with
prayer (like

your ghost like the eucharist
my eyes are open

nets (and any
of Chris and i

second you will swim out
will catch you by the fin (leaping out

of the TV (if i hold on (if i keep
my face against the god

watching your old videotapes with
damn screen (

i'll get
i'll understand why

you.
you left (

eyes open, i dive into the shallow
open, i sit in your movie

end of this video (eyes
like old water (Chris sits in me

and we weep because
with us (let this cup

you aren't laughing
pass (oh lord

i hate this drink
i hate this drink

i'll have another,
i'll have it all

0.

you left i won't let you leave

SELF-INJURY HEALING RITUAL

0.
PENETRATING INJURIES: GUNSHOT:
KEEP IN MIND BULLETS BOUNCE OFF
BONE PATH HARD TO PREDICT   E X I T
WOUND   ALWAYS   LARGER   THAN
ENTRANCE   COULD BE THE SIZE OF YOUR
MOUTH OR KEYBOARD OR THE LAKE OF
YOUR DEPRESSION

0.
FACIAL FRACTURES: REMOVE AND SAVE
LOOSE   TEETH   AND   BONE   FRAGMENTS
FROM THE MOUTH AND TRANSPORT WITH
YOU OK KEEP DISLODGED   TEE
TH TEETH   TEE
TH   IN

A CONTAINER OF PATIENT'S SALIVA OR
MILK IF POSSIBLE OH LORD HOW DO I LIVE
IN   A BODY THAT DOESN'T WANT ME IN
IT   IF   POSSIBLE   FILL   PAPER   WITH
WORDS THAT ARE SALIVA OR MILK AND
BIG ENOUGH TO HOLD ALL OF YOU AND
YOUR DEAD AND ALIVE FRIENDS   OK
HOLD TIGHT IF YOU LET GO IT CANT BE
REATTACHED   HOLD   ALL   OF   THEM
AND YOU IN THIS PAPER   HOLD IT UP
AGAINST YOUR FACE AND   DON'T LOOK
AWAY UNTIL YOU SEE   HOW IT CAME
OFF   HOW IT CAN BE
REATTACHED

0.
ANXIETY WORSENS HEAD INJURY   KEEP
PATIENT CALM AND QUIET

0.
TREAT   LOW   GLUCOSE   LEVELS
AGGRESSIVELY

O.

Richard, what's happeniii-

−Chris Farley
(as Tommy
Callahan III

CHRIS FARLEY'S NAVY BLUE BLAZER

(
Ohhh ok, I see.   It's funny: how   I   sit
still only when   I'm eating.

(
Chewing is another kind of laughter and I see why,
Christopher, you eat icing straight off the tv screen.
Why you cut the cake with your hand. Why lick the
white paint off your own face. Why call the white on
your gums vanilla. Why the expensive jacket on an
expensive body on a poor kid (We all want to feel ok.

I get it, I do. Your death's an SNL skit my friends
quote verbatim. Chris, I've seen your video a hundred
times. I get the joke:

(
See, it's like you're my tailor and I'm yours. Trying
our material on. Like, in stitches. More lines than
Charlie Sheen's breakfast haha. Oh wait you're not
laughing   [hits himself]   GOD. I'm such an idiot.

Sorry, I wear this Chris costume like a method actor.
New one over the old, caking you on. Ya know, like
how you fit into Matt Foley and Tommy Callahan like
coat sleeves? Rising into each skinny arm like yeast,
like the TV's a hot oven? That classic bit about how
actors get big overnight. But you're not bread so, uh,
wait   [hits himself]   GOD I'm so stupid. Sorry.

Uhhh. Oh ok. Ya know how Wisconsin is God and
his laughter is snow and, like, your open jaw's a snow
shovel? And, it's like, you have to haul yourself out of
yourself? Haha yeah you, uh, you remember when
you yelled in that movie? Yeah. That was awesome.

(
Hey, hey, you know Robin Williams? Haha yeah my
Dad looks exactly like him and uh, wait, no I don't
like this joke. Oh, I got it. Ya know how the pope

says when you die you go to heaven? Well when you die in heaven you come back as a comedian. Heyo.

Ok the gag goes like: a comedian swan dives into a dive bar   (and out of himself   (out of the velvet curtains of the Tonight Show   (onto Leno's polished floor   (through a coffee table   (then a bunk bed   (chair (chair   (guts of the world like cake   (a tiny blue blazer (morphine   (is a stage and the lights only get brighter (warmer   (hugs tight around the elbow ditch   (like the laughing mouths of America's boys   (a wedding ring around your whole forearm   (the tv   (a coat you grow bigger than   (but not out of   (haha you remember that scene? That was awesome.

(
Uh huh, I get it. Yeah yeah grief or whatever. Ok I'll go through it again:

You know how if you explain the joke, you kill the joke. Then what are these lines and lines of explaining if not coke. Heart disease. Ohhh, which explains why the cokeheads in high school would kick the shit out of me (they were only trying to explain something: me. To me. Fat. But funny. Chris Farley,

you explain me as 'friend'. You explain me and
my dead friend and I don't know you at all. But I
have to explain you to understand him. You. Like a
euphemism, a dad joke, a pun, a costumed word, a coat
split clean in two (you and I. And by 'you' I mean I, and
by that I mean 'fat kid who loves his dead heroes and
hates himself. Who got thin' but not really 'thin'. More
like 'good at disappearing.'

(
You see? That's the point. You say 'needle' and it's, like, a pun. You hold a needle but you're really holding you (thin, upside down, bright snow. You are weightless. Sinking slow through a coffee table. But actually through you. Actually the back door

of a comedy club. You leave like laughter out of an angry god's mouth. Like, ya know, how laughter is worship and we all want some angry god to like us. And by 'god' I mean 'all of us.' And by 'us' I mean you. You want to laugh at yourself because laughing means breathing, which means living, and we're all so fucking out of breath it's funny. We're taking your cue. We want to be laughter and by that I mean invisible and loud and loved and here but on the way out. Or whatever. Cue laugh track.

(

You remember when you laughed so hard you threw up? How it was the same thing. Like laughter, but vomit? Encore onto hotel carpet? Back into your throat like a rerun? It's an old gag. Yeah, you killed on the night haha get it? No? (Ok back to the video:

Ok you're watching Robin watching Rodney do his tie gag (anxiously adjusting it (and look it's you (in your jacket (its seams opening (its sides splitting (mouthing your best line ('stick around we'll be right back' (its warm sleeves (the laughing mouths of America's kids (its gold buttons (are their eyes (bright cameras (you see? (how (for you (we gleam gleam gleam (we think you're gold, Mister Farley (awesome (good stuff (it's a really good bit

(

No? Nothing? Ok, look at yourself again. Still doesn't make sense? You don't get it? Yeah, I don't either. But I actually do. I get it I don't get it. I get it, yeah, I don't get it. But I get it. I do. I know every line of your death by heart and I still don't get it. Anyways, you see it's like:

Well that's my time. You've been a great crowd, thank you. Thank you. Thanks thanks thanks. I mean it. Thank you. Oh no, thank you. Ok then, yeah thanks, I'm here till Wednesday, tip your waiter, try the veal. Catch you at the buffet   (

THE OTHER HALF OF THE COAT

)
oh shit. sorry Chris. i did it again. this one's boiling
over its belt, another blazer split clean in two like us.
so so sorry, i wanted to be well-contained. but my
eyes are bigger than my plate and all these words
words words keep landing on the page and, Chris, i
don't know how to say no. i will always only be my
body of work, and all it does is stress eat.
ok fuck it. keep the cake coming:

1. ok 'fat guy in a little coat'
1. uh yeah, line like 'the empty plate says god's not angry
   with you, he's bored of you. which i think is worse'
1. ok 'van down by the river'. we laugh. but won't watch you go home to it
   don't know by 'van' you mean you
   (but i do. i live in a you too
1. wait, weight, white lines about being a fat kid
1. uhhh oh how i went through high school hogtied in my own hoodie, round
   the throat, cue panic attack
   (o god Robin Rodney help me breathe
1. ok ok how i used to hallucinate and the ghost of Hercules
   would touch my flab. he told me how he too was eaten by his own clothes
1. i'd dream of Robin and Rodney and god dunking us
   underwater. we're dying. we're not graceful about it
1. keep talking ok how i pissed the sheets until sixth grade and woke up in
   weird places standing up
1. and somehow this helps me understand dead comedians
1. how i wear my heroes and hope i'm more than how i'll die.
   how i'm not afraid to die, i'm afraid of going quiet. how i howl for a
   living (for five years i i i howl into this book and ask you to read it (yeah ok
   like we don't all hurt (like my hurt is special
1. oh shit how the seams on Hercules open like a limp jaw
1. oh shit how this paper opens up to broadcast the ugly Hamlet inside
1. fat guy in New York falls through coffee table. fat kid in Houston falls
   through Catholic school (i eat your videos with my eyes and you go through
   me and for two hours i am clean inside. i watch you and i am not sick
1. ok You as Chris Farley as Hamlet: 'Hath opened his ponderous and marble
   jaws / to cast thee up again'
1. Chris as Hamlet's clown holding up death to our eyes like 'holy schnikes,
   don't look:

1. don't imagine the interior of Kennedy's Lincoln. or the poor comedian who had to clean it
1. or 'depression is a beehive.' or Chris laughing honey into my pill bottle
1. or Daffy Duck dropping his rifle to catch his own bill in his hands. it's ok the gun's a cartoon the blood's a cartoon the jaw can be put back on my friend's still alive we're just watching a bad movie
1. it's ok it's fine i'll change the channel
1. 'hey Dad, I can't see real good: is that Bill Shakespeare over there?'
1. i cover my dad and friends with the icing of comedy, and the only honest talks i have are with videos of dead comedians
1. pitylaughs are another kind of prayer and we are its patron saints etc
1. the only friend i had growing up. us, quoting your movies like loudmouthed rosaries
1. a hundred ways to tell the only joke we know:
1. the pratfall, the pitylaugh
1. i hadn't seen you in years and i'm scared i'll still take your cue. i still look up to you, pratfalling off a roof, out of my mouth. i still quote you quoting Chris i can't watch our favorite movies anymore without weeping eating repeating lines about your suicide because i can't let you be dead. i quote You as Matt Foley as Erasure Poem:
1. 'you, kid, are gonna go out and get the world and wrap it around you. you're gonna end in a river'
1. Mikey, i didn't lose all that weight until i lost you. i'm so sad i'm still hungry
1. most people watch this horrible world from the couch. but Mikey we ate it up with our forehead kissing the goddamn screen. we sunk into the static like a cake knife. whatever. we both had enough of life but i have to clean this plate. i want want want to say 'done. ok i'm done now'
1. leave early. ok Irish goodbye. don't wait for applause. leave it open-ended like a jaw. i don't know, like:
1. 'hey listen to your clapping hands that's the sound of boys throwing themselves through tables from various heights'
   (

O.

I am not here.
I was not here.

—Altar of Plagues

HIGH FALL HEALING RITUAL

0.

PROCEDURE: HIGH FLOW O2 15 L/MIN
THRU NRB BLOOD GLUCOSE IF ALTERED
MENTAL STATE THINK HYPOGLYCEMIA
MEDCOMPLICATIONSINTOXICANTSDRUG
OD ALCOHOL HALLUCINOGENS ETC
OXYGEN AND GLUCOSE IMPORTANT TO
BRAIN FIRST THINGS YOU SHOULD THINK
OF ASK IF SUFFICIENT O2 AND SUGAR

0.

FALL FROM 15 FEET OR 3 TIMES PATIENT'S
HEIGHT IS 'SERIOUS' GET PATIENT
HISTORY AND ANY ANSWERS FROM FAMILY
OR FRIENDS IF POSSIBLE HAVE
AUTHORIZED PERSONNEL IN AMBULANCE
WITH YOU FOR YOUR SAFETY NEVER LET
YOUR GUARD DOWN DIFFUSE AND
CONTROL SITUATION SAFELY TRANSPORT
INTERVENE ONLY AS MUCH AS IT TAKES IF
1+ DEAD ASSUME SERIOUS INJURIES IN
OTHERS OH LORD ITS EASY TO BE
NOTHING

0.

ASSESS FROM A DISTANCE IS PATIENT
HOLDING OR NEAR UNSAFE OBJECTS DOES
PATIENT HAVE LARGE ALCOHOL/DRUG
INTAKE AIR OF DEEP DESPAIR SLOW
SPEECH SEEM AS IF THEY AREN'T REALLY
THERE IS PATIENT UNABLE TO TALK
ABOUT THE FUTURE ASK PATIENT IF THEY
HAVE VACATION PLANS IS PATIENT'S
SPEECH LOUD OBSCENE ERRATIC BIZARRE
INDICATES EMOTIONAL DISTRESS IS
ENVIRONMENT UNSAFE FOR EXAMPLE
OPEN WINDOW IN HIGH-RISE
OR PATIENT ON BRIDGE OR PRECIPICE OR
DOING CIRCLES OVERHEAD O LORD ITS
EASY TO BE NOTHING FALLS

FROM 15 FEET ARE CONSIDERED 'SERIOUS'
AS ARE REPEATED DROPS INTO
QUESTIONABLE WATER EVEN IF PATIENT
DOESN'T SEEM 'SERIOUS' OR CLAIMS
OTHERWISE KEEP IN MIND ANYTHING
COULD INDICATE CRY FOR HELP
INTERVENE IMMEDIATELY EVEN VAGUE
SUGGESTIONS SHOULD NOT BE TAKEN
LIGHTLY EVEN IF PRESENTED AS A JOKE
EXAMPLE:

1.
'hey i'm worried about you. i can cancel stuff and
drop by. i was just gonna day drink and listen to
doom metal anyways'

'haha i'm ok but thanks <3 go listen to Thou and
drunk text me and don't ever die ok good talk haha
but really   hey   h   e   y
seriously   i s w e a r   t   o   god
                    don't   you fucking die ok
                                        i got next

THE CEMENT WHISPERS TO DUSTIN

0.
SEE: THE STITCHES 'MY BABY HATES ME'
SEE: DUSTIN   DOLLIN,   20-YEAR   OLD
AUSTRALIAN PRO SKATEBOARDER

0.
Dustin, you're up:
you pissdrunk angel
in a blazer, gliding
down a gold twenty-stair handrail, break-
ing your arm yet again
like a harp string under a hammer.
Your eyebrow stitches open up and sing

('BARTENDER, BARTENDER   BRING ME
ANOTHER DRINK   SCOTCH BOURBON OR
WHISKEY   I DON'T WANNA THINK'

Your forearm
bends the wrong way and you laugh.
What the fuck are you
if not a ragdoll. Dollin,
if there is a stairway to heaven
I bet you black out halfway up.

0.
Oi! You Jim Beam tumbling down my hoarse throat.
Oi! Oi! Vitruvian Man with gin & tonic
and ankle full of screws
and unpaid hospital bills.
Oi! You dapper drunk, your piss makes a fine pomade.
I run you through my hair, you comb of broken wrists.
You mop of black hair dye,
wiping up the Gold Coast cement with your cheekbone,
licking   glass   outta   your   hand   like   it's   the   bottom   of   a   highball.

0.
This fucking hospital is a bear trap, Dustin. Respectfully decline! If they try to
put a cast on your big mouth, take a handsaw to the bastard! Eat the alcohol
swabs out of their cabinets! Knock back a Clorox bottle! Piss in the ER! You

don't have to be able to walk outta here (that's why you have a skateboard, asshole. It's a punkgurney and it's yours. So roll away again like you actually have somewhere to

go (ok I know you don't. Except 'out back.' Ok go there. I've seen you in this alley before, break   ing a fifth of Bundy against that cement wall that is your name. Dustin, it's even prettier when

0.
you are the bottle.
I want to see you throw yourself against Oz.
Want to see you crack. Want to see your shards bloom all over Bris Vegas.
You bouquet of boneroses, leave your glasspile body at the front door.
You like my haircut? It's called Dustin (high and tight and a fucking mess haha.
The only 12 steps we know are from the ER to the liquor store huh?
Dustin, So Cal teens are rolling themselves, livers and all, under your wing's
cast.
Sons of addicts at last see how fucking rad their parents are.
Thank you Dustin!
With you, we kneel at the altar of Fuck and offer
up our baby teeth.

0.
Our angel, you get
up those god–
damn stairs and fall back
down.
Oi! Oi! Dustin, again!
You better black out
like that winking hole in your shit-eating grin,
like your hole head's a bloody mouth, repeating:

      ('BARTENDER, BARTENDER   BRING ME
     ANOTHER DRINK   I DON'T WANNA BE
     HERE   AND I CAN'T SEEM TO LEAVE'

     (

BOO BOO CHECKS IN AT THE GOLDEN FLEECE HOTEL & CASINO

(hi, i'm here for the wedding or whatever. you guessed it: i'm the groom. or wait no i'm the minister. or 'that guy on the floor' or the 1940's or the i don't know. oh, usher. right, i am usher. usher guy. i am adult. hey question:

(i heard there are actual angels in this hotel? and they strut through the halls like holy fucking peacocks? in hot glue, feathers, fire, and pumps blessed with holy water? you know Pimebomb and Fremont and Tongueclick and Heartdisease and Heroine (Heroin?) and how they make kissyfaces at ya and melt ya like a birthday candle? Whew! i wanna die. and get born again in goddamn lights and i'm gonna uh huh it's state law. gonna cash out this heart and get a handsome neon one. oh hey:

(how do I sundaybest? does this blood match my belt? can i use antidepressants as cufflinks? can i shake my pop's hand with a prescription? can i bring my medicine cabinet as a plus one? hey can i use this pill bottle as a kaleidoscope? will it make this world look like champagne? will everything be wine? my blood too? how about this straight edge? will it bubble up in my hand like a flock of geese? will i? am i a good thing to look at? here, rest your forehead against my glass: see something worth opening? yeah? you know where wine bubbles come from? you got it: imperfections in the glass. hey am i champagne or a forty? i bet i'm a forty. hey:

(how do i usher? this wine into me? quick enough? how do i wave how do i glow i wanna glow hey how do i toast? can i do it in this chair? do i have to put down my drink? can i usher with this flask? carry you in it and keep you safe? walk you into a holy place? am i Virgil or Charon or just a burnt-out EMT? have i ever helped anyone? have i done anything worth dressing up for goddammit? hey:

(all stories are supposed to end in a wedding or funeral right? guess this ain't my story huh? who's wedding is it again? oh it is mine? i'm getting married? to someone i hate? i'm marrying me? again? this is best day of my life. wow, thanks. thanks thanks thanks. hey:

(how do I usher me out of myself? can i write these vows with a cake knife? cut the cake of my glut groin depression bachelor lines yeah cut off my own bloody leg like a bouquet of roses and offer it up to Six-Pack God? how come i reach into my gut and pluck a flower of fat and then two more grow in its place? is all this air going to my hips? i can hold my breath. i only need one lung right? if this soul is 21 grams how many pounds is that and can i cut it off?

(i don't want to eat. being alive hurts. i hate it in me, it's too hot. my guts marathon out of my body and i let them go. oh Dysmorphia, Greek god i've never even seen, i carve your image from my fat. i give you myself on expensive chinaware. i eat myself sick and run circles till i write your name in vomit. i trace a big 0 over and over till i become it. Gorgeous, like you. i want to become you and you aren't even here   (you don't even exist   (which means you are a good place to rest (hey   (i'm so tired (hey heyhey [gasp] hey:

(you have beds here in Lake Charles? yeah but not for me? i sleep in the buffet? oh the wedding's not even here in town? is it in Happy? or Wail? or God's Glass? or Vicodin? hey you been to Vicodin before? oh you gotta go. they have this bakery there where they bake handkerchiefs garters veils whatever. ovens full of them rising like yeast or ghosts. you can eat for years and still be hungry yeah you can crawl into an oven yourself. you really have to look into it. oh you gotta check out:

(	the Hotel Lobby	that hangs high above the
	Earth.	you climbed up there?
	looked down? seen	the waters of Want over–
	flow our bath,	lick us up,
	gold house	and all. while
	you ask god or the gulls	to scoop us up
	in their holy beaks	but they don't.
	you up there	with them. you watch us
	kick	and kick the water
	kissing our foreheads	like a young mom
	each splash	sounding like:
	I	*I*
	I	am so thirsty.

(yeah yeah i see the line. christ. ok one last thing: i wanna check out. yes this early. oh i'm not allowed? to usher myself out? oh i have to hang on? oh, wait here till i die? o it gets better?   o, o it'll be ok? o.

DROWNING INJURY HEALING RITUAL

0.

LARYNGOSPASMS: COUGH LOOKS LIKE
CHOKING SUPINE POSITION ARTIFICIAL
VENTS WITH MOUTH TO MOUTH OR
POCKET MASK PACKAGE PATIENT TO
BUOYANT BACKBOARD WITH RESTRAINTS
REMOVE FROM WATER COVER WITH
BLANKET O2 CPR OPEN AIRWAY WITH
HEAD TILT CHIN LIFT OR JAW THRUST OH
LORD ITS EASY TO BE EVERYTHING AND
NOTHING UNDERWATER OK EXPLAIN THIS
CUP IS YOUR DEPRESSION OK SIT AT THE
BOTTOM AND WAIT TO GROW GILLS:

0.

YOUR THERAPIST WILL ASK ANY VACATION
PLANS   ANYTHING   YOU'RE   LOOKING
FORWARD TO THIS YEAR   DO   YOU
SEE YOURSELF GOING ANYWHERE FUN
HERE WE GO OK DON'T THINK OF YOUR
EMS BOOK   OR   ITS   DEFINITION   OF
'ASPIRATION' OR YOUR PATIENT CHOKING
ON HIS TONGUE OR YOU WEEPING IN THE
BATHROOM OR WHATS IN YOUR COAT OR
YOU PISSDRUNK IN CLASS OH GOD DONT
RELAX INTO THE ROOM YOU FAT TONGUE
DON'T DIP INTO THE DEATHWAVE LIKE
GULF TRASH   'ASPIRATION' CAN ALSO
MEAN HOPE YOU ASSHOLE DONT BE SO
GODDAMN DARK OK LIGHTEN UP OK
DON'T AIR IT ALL OUT WE DON'T WANT TO
HEAR HOW YOU'RE SAD YOU'RE HUMAN
NOT A LUNGFISH AND CAN'T BREATHE IN
AND OUT   OF WATER AND CAN'T LOOK
FORWARD WITHOUT LOOKING DOWN AT
DEATH   BETWEEN YOUR TOES   LIKE
SAND   OK SMILE OK INHALE OK SAY:

1.

the beach

i see myself
at the beach

with everyone i love

diving

I DON'T WANT TO WANT (TO DIE)

( )
An airplane mechanic in Houston says he restores 8,000 lbs bibles because his machines will lift you high as heaven. He presses grease on his tongue, rivets his hands together and his knees to the hangar floor, and every hour prays to God to let his arms become propellers oh lord let him fly:

( )
The most unbelievable part of this parable is not that it actually happens: that God comes through and the man flies from Galveston to the Vatican in one shot. No. It's the gratitude he feels up in the air. That he does not then wish to become Wind itself, and then Sun, and then the whole goddamn Milky Way, and that his heavy, heavy Want does not drag him into the Atlantic (as he begs God for arms to swim:

( )
ok i climb up my ambulance:
ok i climb up a soul singer:
ok up Chris Farley:
ok up my grandpa:
ok up the benzo bottles:
up Louisiana's catfish and chemical plants:
up depressing internet videos (i eat them like cornbread. i go:
up the refrigerator:
up a bleach bottle:
up my bed and my bed and bed:
up my anxiety until my arms fall off and then i keep going:
up myself and perch on my own:
head like a lopsided crown:
too gorgeous to afford and:
up on high, i draw:
a medicine cabinet into the air:
below and dive down into:
it openmouthed and:
oh god it's all over:
me:
the Heaven:
the light:
has shark teeth:
it eats me:
up (oh god i hate this get me out

A WEDNESDAY NIGHT

0.

If you're just tuning in, the prizefight goes on but the headline has already been written: 'Hammerhead Will Kelly Fights Himself On Live Television & Loses.' Yes sirree, all that's left here is the photo and long ten count. Correspondents have arrived from far and wide to report on tonight's knockdown dragout. The arena tonight is to the rafters in cheering fans with mouths full up with camera flash, folks. Just look at those halogens pop!

You betcha, Will's demons have come with cameras and have the best seats in the house: inside Will's eyes. His eyes tonight are aquariums and his demons have swelled up against the glass. It's easy to spot: Will is currently looking out from his knuckles as he floats to his corner now at the end of round 12.

Have a look at him work: yes our featherweight champ is known and highly di-laudid for acting as his own cutman. And again, Will works the bruise away from the eye,
down
into his
mouth.

0.

And there's the bell, as we enter unlucky round 13
Hammerhead Will off the ropes with a hot blast of tired Irish arms.
Will slouching back,
Will testing the air.
The two Wills opening up, exchanging blows.
Hammerhead Will looking
top heavy,
like a reed fat with sugar.
Hammerhead's arms like jellyfish.
Will leaning on Will,
Will on Will's hull like rust,
Will's slowdancing through a room of Vaseline,
Will kissing Will deep,
Xanax under tongue
and Tiger balm on his lips
and onto Will's eyes!
Will goes blind!
Will's eyes are bloated fish!
They beat against the dry hull of the room!

Will with a hook
Will with a hook
Will opens up
Will opens up
Will with the one-two and
Will takes a

0.
dive!
Hammerhead Will sinks through a room of lightbulbs!
Like a hammer!
Like whalefall!
1! 2!
The cameras swim in like hagfish!
With buckets of flash! They pour it on him!
The boxing ring is a giant highball!
4! 5!
Hammerhead Will sucking on the bottom rope!
Will peers through blubber!
Eyes growing fatter than his gloves!
6! 7!
He finds his demons under the lids!
He looks at them and sees stars, coral, pills, halogens,
amphipods!
His anger is glowing shrimp! It makes a home of him!
Will takes a shot at his demons but can't land a hit underwater!
9! 10!

0.
Our heavyweight champ takes a cab home from the hospital!
Will showers blind and has dinner for 1!
2! Boy oh boy, Will opens his fat eyes with a fish hook!
1! Will empties cough syrup into his glove and whales on himself!
Will squares off with a fist full of Ativan and wins!
He works himself into bed like a bruise! Lays back like canvas decoration! Ears
ringing like year-long bell!
1! Will fights his anxiety on live TV every day! He telegraphs every punch!
1! Will writes about boxing himself and loses!
1! Will tries to pray and loses!
His demons have the longer reach!
1! Will tries to open his fist!
Will can't quite open his fist!

O.

As if the gods were bored with peace in our hearts.
And their fingers are itchy.

—Mgła

I saw lions and leopards and wolves,
and they howled and roared around me.

—Dante

ANIMAL INJURY HEALING RITUAL

0.

NO EXIT   WOUND IF IT COMES TO REST
ON INSIDE SIGNS: OIL FOUNDATION IN
FEATHERS WATERLOGGED WINGS AIR OF
DEEP DESPAIR   REMOVE   PATIENT
FROM POISONOUS ENVIRONMENT   IF
POSSIBLE

0.

ENVIRONMENTAL EMERGENCY: MARINE
ANIMALS: LIMIT   DISCHARGE   OF
NEMATOCYSTS   BY   AVOIDING   FRESH
WATER WET SAND SHOWERS CARELESS
MANIPULATION   OF   TENTACLES   AND
MOTION OF AFFECTED LIMB   KEEP
PATIENT   CALM   INACTIVATE
NEMATOCYSTS WITH VINEGAR AND MEAT
TENDERIZER SCRAPE   OFF REMAINING
TENTACLES WITH EDGE OF STIFF OBJECT
SUCH AS A CREDIT CARD OR DEATH METAL
CD   SNAKE BITE: PROCEDURE: BLS
FOR   RESPIRATORY   DISTRESS   RAPID
TRANSPORT TO ER FOR MUSCLE RIGIDITY
CALM   PATIENT   AVOID   MOVEMENT
GENTLY CLEAN BITE AREA WITH SOAPY
WATER DO NOT APPLY ICE CHECK VITALS
MARK SKIN WITH A PEN AND NOTE IF IT
CONTINUES TO   S   W   E   L

1.

L   LEAVE ANY FOREIGN OBJECT IN EAR
FOR PHYSICIAN TO REMOVE

1.

LORD HOW DO I LIVE IN A WORLD THAT
DOESNT WANT ME IN IT

1.

IF POSSIBLE BRING THE SNAKE

GODORANGE

1.
It's ok. Ok?

This isn't happening   (I am dreaming

of a Bible,   or an orange peel

(I don't know which.   It keeps changing

(But it doesn't matter   ok? Ok,

1.
I'm in an orange grove. Valencias.   A young
woman, with black hair and wet pulp grin, offering
me her other half.   And then it changes:

the girl and her orange   are now young David,
hoisting Goliath's head up to God's lips like ripe
fruit. Heaven has a tongue.   Everything   changes
again:

Heaven is morning light on a white ceiling. Goliath's
head is my head. David is now my depression   and
then a roach   and then both.   I hear the Sun
peel–   no an orange–   I hear either a loud Sun
or loud Orange peeling open but it's actually my
eardrum and insect teeth and tsktsktsk

(To the layman, the East Texas Suicide Letter often
appears to be an arthropod: household   roach,
ladybug, what have you.   It enters the ear canal
while its host is asleep   (Your Anxiety, being
an insect, is wont to claw its way up to your eardrum
and talk (but it's ok   (ok?   (It isn't
really happening

(I won't repeat what the roach is saying to me
(except that he calls me

Goliath   (And then I become

Goliath:

1.

I who defy Your holy king.   I, bruised Godorange,
who spits his bitter pith at Your heaven. I whose
ugly is six cubits high. Gaze upon Goliath:

(in his living room   (in his underwear   (hunched
over and crying and clutching his ear like a shield
(raving about a   David   inside his head! King
I Hate Myself walks openly across this brain like it's
Goliath's dead body (Lord, surely you hath hand-
delivered me into the lion's jaw:

Both Heaven and Depression have teeth. They have
a throat. I have a big blood orange head   (and then
it changes:

King Anxiety is a hungry insect. It wants to eat and
eat   (and then it changes: King
Lonely   is an ER nurse   (gorgeous   (legs for
days. And I say 'unhh he's   in there   e a t e a t
ing up my head like a blood orange'   (And
you say 'Ok ok honey, move your hand. Let me
look. Oh sorry. All I see is blood'   (And I say
'Goddammit yeah. I bet you do:

0.

yeahyeah ya know when my head is bible   all   i
see is blood! when my head Goliath all i feel are
Davids   hands in my hair when   m y   h e a d
slingstone i feel you Nurse cuppin   m y   c h i n
like a clementine andand when   i ripe clementine
all i dream is knives! and when   my hands is knives
all i wanna do is cut this head into slices and ask you
to eat the lonely outta me and when   i w a k e u
p wantin to kill myself   i hear your legs Nurse:
why ur leg so loud?   c u t c u t t i n u p m y

ear   canal?   whats with all the O
J upup your thigh 'n   my lip:

(yea i have head is   bible again and is   o r a n g e
again and is human   skull again and then   b i b l e
orange skull bible   orange skull   bibleorangeskull
bibleorangeskull   and ohhh ok ok   (i s e e:

how hhow all three are exactly alike   (because of
how ofhow much they bleed   (ohhh o k:
howw ow you have to open each one   with a knife:

0.
oh god Goliath now look upon these words: this
is very ugly.   they will not draw   us,   like
David.   they will not love   us,   ugly
Goliath.   we have let boxcutters and insects
further   in than anyone we love   (ugly!
the ideas i have allowed well into this Head (uglyugly!
Head, have i.   i,   hateit   i
hatethis Head   iwanna   take   it
off   (and then i do:

i am holding my Head in front of me   (it changes
into a cup then keyboard then back into my Head:
(i reach in and clean the bad thoughts   out   ok:

(i am holding in my hand   an   insect.

it changes into   a   wedding ring.

And then   an   orange   seed,

already sprouted. And then   a   little   sun,

leaking citrus. And then   Vicodin Lidocaine

sling and stone and then just   an earful of blood

(It doesn't matter   (It really doesn't

0.

Ok,   an orange.
i am holding   an orange. Ok now

i am holding   words:
'Clementine'   'O my darlin'

'It's ok. It's   out now. Shh,
I got it   out.

O
k?'

HEAD INJURY HEALING RITUAL

0.
REMEMBER: EXIT WOUND WILL BE LARGER
THAN ENTRANCE   TOXINS MAY
BREAK FREE INTO   BLOOD   IF
ALLOWED TO SIT IN BODY

0.
INJURY TO NECK AND THROAT: SERIOUS IF
TRACHEA TORN/SWOLLEN   USE ROLLER
GAUZE TO SECURE DRESSING IN PLACE DO
NOT WRAP BANDAGE AROUND NECK C-
COLLARS ARE GOOD PRESSURE DRESSINGS
BUT IF PAPER IS ALL YOU HAVE AT HAND
WELL KNOCK YOURSELF   OUT
ASSESSMENT: IRREGULAR RESPIRATIONS
LOW LOC RACCOON EYES BATTLES SIGN
VISUAL COMPLAINTS   A B N O R M A L
BEHAVIOR NAUSEA   V O M I T I N G
CONFUSED/SLURRED SPEECH SOME WILL
HAVE NO OBVIOUS SIGNS   ASSESS FOR
SHOCK   HIGH FLOW O2 THRU NRB
MASK   DO NOT ATTEMPT TO STOP
BLEED   APPLIED PRESSURE MAY CAUSE
BLOOD TO POOL IN HEAD   LIGHTLY WRAP
HEAD WITH DRESSING   KEEP SITE STERILE
ALWAYS RISK OF INFECTION TO BRAIN   IF
SKULL FRACTURE DRESSING WILL SHOW
YELLOW STAIN AROUND BLOOD LIKE A
TARGET OR HALO   IF YOUR BRAIN'S
BROKE LOOK AT YOURSELF YOU LITTLE
CIRCLE IN YOUR GAUZE   BED   YOUR
ANXIETY A YELLOW HALO   G L E A M I N G
TRY HARD TO EDIT IT   OFF AT THE
NECK AND HOPE   TWO   MORE
DON'T GROW BACK   WHERE   THE
OLD ONE   WENT

0.
ANXIETY WORSENS HEAD INJURY   K E E P
PATIENT CALM AND QUIET

BARSALONEA

<pre>
                    0.   0.
gemini,   i   know   it's heavy.
hauling   around two   heads   on   shoulders   only
big   wide enough for   one.
h   o   l   d   on:

                    0.   0.
every morning, i wake up at 6,   walk to my bathtub, and sit at the
edge. i keep a kitchen knife   there by my medication. my
twin's head will get out a   word or two like 'Barsalonea'
'Oh God' 'Wedding Cake'   before i take the knife and cut his
throat.   i   begin   to   remove   the   whole

                    0.   0.
h   e   a   d   i
work   the   knife   quick   while   he   quiely   weeps
(he's   a   violin   with   warm breath and a lot of blood.
it   takes   about   an   hour   only because
i've   gotten   really   good   at it.
i   get   it   done   and get dressed

                    0.   0.
(i   already   hold   enough.
in this head (i can't have   two of them. it's too

                    0.   0.
                    heavy

                    0.
                    (hold on
                    hold on

              (i'm almost through the bone
</pre>

FOR GODSAKE IF YOU KILL YOUR DARLINGS YOU GOTTA DO SOMETHING ABOUT THE BODIES

(
the other 'Bill Moran' on the internet is a well-respected bladesmith and my words don't gleam or cut like his knives do so here: all the shit i couldn't empty out because i'm garbage and don't know how to say   go- go- byego- good-   go go-bye dye   goodbyee:

1.
ok i couldn't keep people alive so i take up taxidermy and wow it comes easy   i keep the dead around like a champ   shine 'em like trophies   i'm not even trying haha i'm that good:

1.
i clean Death like a trout. i dress this paperdeer quicker than i dress myself. i crawl into the computer like a caterpillar, come out a butterfly   knife:

1.
ok if origami cranes bring long life what animal will help me die young? give me a get-well card and a swill of Powers, i'll fold that shit with my mouth:

1.
i'll make an origami me. i'll make 1000 of them. i'll tie 'em on a string for you:

1.
Todaiji Temple, the 'Buddha's Nostril': a two-foot 'O' cut clean through a wooden support beam. The guide explains the myth: 'go all the way through, and you'll gain free entry into Heaven ok (but don't assume you won't get stuck and panic   ok (at this point we're on a first-name basis with the fire department' ok so i kneel and square up and lean into it like:

0.

an oven and i swell in the belly (holy hell i can't go
through this oh god i'm dying i'm dante dead tree
paper bird taxidermy tourist in my own body here i'm
handing back my ticket Virgil heaven's too goddamn
expensive:

1.

ok then Cannibal Corpse in Tokyo. audience packed:
a ball of silver fish, a tired eye looking or rolling
up. a circle pit opens up and i go into it:

1.

Tokyo: the day that Michael Jackson died. big crowd
in Yoyogi Park. hundreds either in King of Pop
cosplay or crying in falsetto. Michaels offering their
gloves, Michaels weeping into the sequins. and this
grieftourist doing both. Ok yeah, this: i walk into
the hurt like it's a fish market. i dive into Michael's
wake like a funeral bird. open eyes drooling, open bill
glistening like his famous glove. i moonwalk grief into
my gullet and i'm fucking good at it:

1.

oh yeah, the Merritt quote: 'A wonderful bird is
the pelican   /   His Bill will hold more than his belly
can'   Haha ok what else   can   i   fit:

1.
You

1.
You

oh god

1.
You left i won't let you leave:

YOU AS CHRIS FARLEY AS ERASURE POEM

1.
God.   i'm such an idiot.   sorry   (i wanted to
edit you to the bone (your laughter: 114 pounds. it is
an ax i can't lift but i won't let go of (the pen the pills
the page are all an ax handle and how wildly i swing
(like you're bottled in my body (and i have to cut you
out:

0.
'Chris Farley,   my guest, one of the greatest
God   Sounds. You were awesome when you went
all paper. Really pretty.   Remember?   You   were
supposed to be dead   and uh, there   was   you,
backwards and 'dead'   and,   uh,   everyone
thought that   you   were   dead?
And it was a hoax. God was talking you pretty.'
oh, You still

1.
in here?   You still inside?   [hits himself]
God. i'm so stupid. sorry, sorry i'm not good at this:
being who i've always wanted to be:

                                        You
                                        (lean

                            (loved me then left. went
                                        through:

                            (me like medicine. didn't overstay
                            your welcome: didn't want to haunt

                    (the place.   got the toxin out and got
                    out: a good friend: a good medic

                            (sorry i'm not good at this   ((

86

O.

Physician, heal thyself.

—Zao

*I haven't closed my eyes
in a long time.*

I am trying.

—Gojira

ACTIVATED CHARCOAL HEALING RITUAL

0.

PROCEDURE: YOUR GOAL IS TO REMOVE
THE POISON   REMOVE PATIENT
FROM TOXIC ENVIRONMENT TOXINS MAY
BREAK   FREE INTO BLOODSTREAM IF
ALLOWED   TO   SIT   IN   BODY
CONTRAINDICATIONS: LACK   OF
CONSCIOUSNESS OR GAG REFLEX   SYRUP
OF IPECAC IS UNADVISED AS PATIENT
COULD INHALE VOMITUS INTO LUNGS
AVG DOSE CHARCOAL 1 GM PER KG BODY
WEIGHT   MANY WILL VOMIT   TRY
AGAIN EXPLAIN IT'S OK BUT YOU HAVE TO
KEEP IT DOWN   INDICATIONS: POISONS
INCLUDE HOUSEHOLD CLEANERS EXPIRED
FOOD ALCOHOL DRUGS GRIEF COMEDY
HIM AND HIM AND THE OTHER TWO WHO
ALSO DIED ON YOU AND THE TWO YEARS
YOU WANTED TO BE GAUZE ON THE
WORLD   ABSORB THE HURT H O L D
IT FOR US   HOLD US IN OUR   BODIES
HERE AND   ORGANIZED ALIVE CLEAN
ALL   OF   US CLEAN   ALL   CLEAN
FIELD ADVICE: COCA-COLA REMOVES
DRIED BLOOD FROM PAVEMENT BUT IT
WONT LIFT IT BACK INTO THE BODY
BUT GIVE IT A SHOT BOSS   DRINK COKE
IN WORKSHOP AND SIT AND WAIT TO GET
CLEAN INSIDE EVEN THOUGH BLEACH IS
QUICKER AND YOU KNOW IT   G
O THROUGH OLD EMS NOTES RETYPE
EVERY INJURY LAY ACROSS THE PAPER
LIKE GAUZE   HOLD YOURSELF AGAINST
EVERYONE YOU LOST   HOLD YOURSELF
DOWN ON IT   OK YOU HAVE TO HAVE IT
ALL OK   OK YOU HAVE TO HOLD IT
DOWN OK   OK

0.

REASSESS EVERY 5 MIN DOCUMENT IT ALL

I'M GOLFING WITH DAD. I CLOSE MY EYES.

0.

Ok, Vicodin. Ok look at the Vicodin. i need you to
look at the Vicodin. Ok? Keep an eye on the Vicodin.
But also look at the Dilaudid. 49 Vicodin and
Dilaudid inside this guy and you in a uniform in an
ambulance and the Ativan and Haldol and the   oh,
oh hold on   (uhh there's a kid in here: in

(this paper.
who'd let a little kid waltz
out here in
the field?
it's not safe. he could see
some bad stuff

0.

Ok, the Vicodin. Ok eat it with your eyes. Ok grimy
tongue and nice collar. Oh pale kid twitching in a
pink polo. Oh rich kid drugs waltzing through a rich
kid. Oh frat kid huddled in his blankey and the piss
on your ambulance floor. Ok watch this videotape of
your patient, again and again, until you understand
why he's in a polo shirt dying and not golfing   (ok
wait, will anyone help this kid

(out?
he's walking around the page like
it's a golf course,
wrapped in toilet paper, arms
out, claiming
he's me for christsake

0.

Ok anyways, uhhh don't look at him. Look at him:
your patient, a paper you, ripping out his IVs. Look at
his Vicodin, not yours. Him still here, not you. Him.
You be Dante ok? Look back, at yourself, age eight,
golfing with Dad. Ok back to the addict. Ok equal

sign between. Ok zoom in. His eyes, upturned. White circles right? Golf balls in the marsh. Ok Dad's eyes and the math inside. Little Vicodins. An equation in the vomit. White O's white zeroes that organize him and you and O all the bad shit you've seen. Ok write a zero every time you want to die and O,

O,

don't stop writing. O Lord look hard. For what will last of us. Circle it. White rings that will hold us, when our expensive bodies won't. White ring lights to see us through death, see us when we blur and disappear. Anything but O, O, white O's on a price tag, white Vicodin, bright white vomit on a nice shirt   (O goddammit. This kid keeps walking across

(the screen,
making dead boy noises.
OOOOoooh. look at his
bowl cut, his nice shirt under a mummy getup.
(it's so easy
to see: he's me, age 8, and O
my god, i won't
go away. go away
kid. Ok,
get out of
here. O
my god,
go

0.

Ok, sorry everyone. You know, i wanted to do important work here: put the ugly in a polo (with us (like we're all this dying rich kid and i could still heal him ok?   (But O here comes this kid, walking

(in the way, you
know? asking me to let this dead guy let this
dead guy
go and

(O, look
alive and write something new
like i don't have a price to pay
(painkillers to take
(white circles till i die.
he's looking at me with those
little paper eyes
O,   O,
like i'm the addict

0.
What, William? What do you want? Want to be a
medic and help everyone but yourself? You got all
this white paper over you and your eyes and you don't
even see where you're going, but you're walking right

into it. You want to see death and you don't even see
your body: extra large shirt, big O bowl cut, years
ahead to revise yourself like it's Halloween and you're
afraid to be anything alive. i see you in your mummy
costume. Real spooky William, take it off. Before it
sticks. Death is sticky. It'll wear you like fat. It isn't
dark, it's bright. Video static vomit on your

shirt. All other details, lost in the glare. You look at it,
then anything else, and you still look at it. A bright
white polo. Easy on the eyes. Look, i can't look out
for you. i can't cover your eyes. Because i watched a
kid die one time and i still have to organize it. Ok?

(O
god, i want to

0.
rewind
to my first ambulance shift and quit. before

i saw it. got it on my hands and shirt,
got all sticky, got too old to be 28.

i could look at anything. if i wanted, i could
close my eyes   and see:

only
the lids.

i want to forget death on a Sunday.
i want to wear a nice shirt,

golf with Dad,
and not give up halfway.

1.
William come out here on the field,
up on my shoulders, high enough to see:

over me
(i will carry you, if you cover my eyes

(look for us, out of us, into us and tell me:
is there anything holy?

have i even helped anyone?
(Ok, i am closing

my eyelids
(and the eyelids inside my eyes (i see:

white static
white circles

(a hundred, organizing,
into one bright one:

        (O my god,
        it's a sun

      (   )

WALT DISNEY'S NEW CAMERA

0.

'Now, this is a different kind of drawing... the blueprint of a piece of equipment designed to make cartoons more realistic, and enjoyable.'

(
i watched the videotape again / of that dream / where my old deathpoems come alive / and wear the re-animated bodies of Disney characters / and throw a rager in my hot and crowded studio apartment // It's midnight and Mufasa eats old cake out of the trash, that guy with the dogs fishes a Dalmatian hair out of his highball, and i cry and cartoon on my arms // i am hand-drawing / line / by line / the 'I' i want to be by the end of this movie, when live-action / Alive You / walks through / the front door like / your first day / of retirement / Gold clothes / celluloid crown / warm technicolor / You / grin and oh god if my dumb heart had teeth / it'd be grinning too / Cue strings / applause // Walt coughs himself awake in the front hallway / blinks / hovers his 8mm eyes over your oxfords:

the kneeling director leans in: head: upside-down:	goes heel-over-flat as paper: he is a
new, topline, 6-foot new equipment: new angle:	Multiplane camera: on an
old scene: He gets to it: feet and for the rest of the dream:	hovers over my the ghost of
	Walt Disney: up and down,
	up and down: huffing
	onto my shoes. shining them:

KITCHENFIRE

0.

It's an oven in here, in the back of this ambulance.
Our truck's a/c is out. Outside, 121 degrees. At 621
lbs, Mister Horowitz waterfalls on our oversized
gurney with us. We're sweating   bullets. Leaking
like a French beach. Hearts knocking on the front
door of our chests like it's a folded flag and some bad
news:

0.

'Son, i'm sorry about this'
'It's ok, sir. Here's an
ice pack. An
ice pack. An-
other' on his thigh, underarm. i hold
a pillowcase soaked in water and lay
it on his
forehead like it's the ring that held
up a kayoed Son-
ny Liston.

0.

On the windshield, i've a taped a photo of my dad on
his wedding day: velvet bowtie, slice of white cake,
and 600 lbs smile. i see it and suddenly my hands look
so
thin.
So
i

take a piece of paper and write:
'god is a wedding cake.'

i tear it   off and fold it into fours and   e a t :
the words, paper and ink. i   e a t :

1.

'he is a wedding cake. these hands are a knife. but i
dunno how to make the first cut.' i   e a t :

1.
'he's a wedding cake shoved into a kick drum. yes,
you can swipe icing off the top as long as you nod
and hum.' and   e   a   t   :

1.
'i hear you. i got icing on these shoes and a wingtip heart.
no, i dunno how to stop running.' and i   e   a   t   :

1.
Yes, amen. this paper is a kitchen, go in. i'm heaven-
sprint at their microphones, heart first, chewing on a
bunch of lit candlewicks. i saw Paper God in a
burning blankey. Nine-months old with kerosene on
his lips, he said 'Son, pass a fire. Son, spit out those
sparks, you're choking on them. Son, eat your words
they will make you big.   E   a   t   :   '

1.
i am.   I am.   Eating a plate fulla flames on paper.
I'm doing this as kitchenfire as I can. The only way I
know how: like a kid, in the air, hurling cake down at
your house as fast as   I love you. Dad, I eat because I
don't know any diet for a heavy

heart. This one
here: a wingtip
shoe. i'm dying but i am not
dead. i'm getting it resouled and shined:

            1.
            Mister Horowitz,
            Mister Liston,

            how does a man   break
            down like that: go

            gray with
            grace

            How does he
            slow

down.   How am I supposed to?
(I don't   know.

I look at my Dad: he   looks   at
every birthday cake like   it's a headstone, like

candles   clog   his   arteries,   like
he knows   his heart's about to blow

out.
He'll carry his white vanilla head-

stone 'til the day he lays in the
grass and wears it like a

crown. It is
heavy, I know.

1.
Dad, you are 6 going on 68 going on statue. If you
have already started to break,

I hope I break
like you:

Scooping up every little ghost that crumbles off
behind you, hot and brave and excited. You carry
God and Sugar and Us for us. Dad, I am right behind
you,   following. I have my hands full:

1.
of packs

1.
of ice

:

I AM TRYING

(
an old metalhead cries in his mom's basement regrets his life's
dream gathers griefwater onto six strings wails on

tape. a zydeco legend admits he is powerless over
alcohol weeps onto his

accordion. a soul singer's best friends get sober to show her
it can be done her best songs say

it can't. an attendant washes the dead emperor's
robe an attendant wipes blood off the marble

floor. an actor falls on TV like a painkiller through the
pain an actor cleans the world with

comedy. a nurse pumps the actor's stomach (she's a big
fan a young medic looks hard at what Hollywood

won't: what the head looks like
after. to the

(anxious	angels
who see the ugly	guts of the world
the River	of Broken Hands
and don't look	away
who learn its width	and depth and
wade into the ugly	Ugly
legs first	and with baffling grace
accept it	and go to work
organizing	assembling
even as they are	disassembled
hosanna	hosanna
god bless	the Swimmers))

O.

The thirst came on.
It came in waves.
…
You are me now.

—Isis

The good times
are killin' me.

—Nathan Abshire

ACTIVATED CHARCOAL HEALING RITUAL

0.

PROCEDURE: IT'S IMPERATIVE THAT PATIENT DRINK 12-16 GLASSES OF WATER AFTER INGESTING DUE TO RAPID DEHYDRATION MANY DO VOMIT EXPLAIN IT'S OK BUT YOU HAVE TO HOLD IT DOWN IT HAS TO GO THRU YOU YOU HAVE TO DIGEST IT ALL OK LISTEN TO 'CLEARING THE PATH TO ASCEND' IN THE AMBULANCE LIKE ITS THE OCEAN AND FLARE GUN OK YELL YOURSELF BRIGHT AND UP AND OUT OK BEAT YOUR HEAVY WINGS ON THE WATER LIKE APPLAUSE AND TEXT YOUR LOVED ONES EXPLAIN I'M DRUNK BUT ALIVE IN UPPERCASE IN THIS CUP PAPER BATH TV TILE GODBLOOD INFERNO HOUSTON AMBULANCE DEATHMETAL HAUNTED HOUSE BOTTLE BUT NOT ALONE ONLY UP FRONT WITH A TINY TRVE KVLT FOLLOWING OK LEAN INTO IT LIKE A DREAM LIKE YOUR FRIENDS ARE HUNGOVER GODS AND WILL DRINK YOU UP AND OUT THE GRIEFWATER AND CHARCOAL CEILING AND YOU'LL WAKE UP CLEAN AND NEXT TO AN ALIVE FRIEND OR ALIVEYOU LIKE AN ANNIVERSARY GIFT AND MORNING BREATH AND HUMMING A STRANGE NEW SONG LIKE:

1.

'you up? morning. hey open your eyes: i got you this water bottle. the instructions say you suck up the water through this charcoal thingy here, and then it comes out clean. it was expensive so you have to use it ok? hey, i won't let you get sick and die ok? hey i won't let you be alone in this ok? if you have to drink your way out of the water of your depression,

i will hold your cup:

DEAR AMY

0.
'Higher the hair, closer to
God. Amy,

make Him inhale your hairspray.
Hide the drugs in there

good.' The wine whispers, 'Miss
Winehouse, you look

great. But we gotta go
go go:

it's Wednesday night
and the band's waiting.

     It's
     showtime.'

     Amy,
     wake up.

0.

Live from a kitchen called   Rehab: the great
Amy Winehouse. You   enter, clean out
of the dishwasher   with champagne and a
snare drum and the   Amys of my family
drinking backup to you,   the whole band with
broken-dish   earrings   and   you're   up
front.   Your mic's off. It doesn't matter.   A—

Live in '98, yelling in the kitchen, it's:
Amy Winehouse & The Ellic Family,
Amy & Uncle at thirteen on house drums
Amy & Grandpa leaking out the photo album
Amy & The Hundred Amys soaked in my
sister's carpet and A Fresh Handle Of
Amy under her pillow
Amy & A Good Mom & Her Whiny Son
Amy Died In Her Black Hair in my young
hands holding it back
Amy Coming Out like a wedding song
Amy & The Vomit, live between the couch
cushions, live on our church clothes. It's
Amy Winehouse: Live in Heaven's No
No No Lounge, with beehive hair glory and
go go ketamine sound and giant cork
in our front door, relapsing
live from the family I love, with her hit
single:

        'I'm
        So So Sorry'

0.
Amy Winehouse,

I only love four women in this world and
two of them are you.

The alcohol calls them 'Amy'
and they answer to Amy,

alone in your eyes and very sick.
Amy,

wake up.　　　　I'm worried　　　　　　about
the　Amy　who　raised　me.　Her　liver's　gone
gold. She wears it like a halo　I'm　　　afraid
one day she'll disappear into　the dishwasher or
driver's seat with a bottle of You and won't come
out again. In her place,　a　hundred　Amy
Winehouse CDs unopened　like　little　caskets.
I don't want you two to meet　(Lord let her stay
a—

0.

Live,　　　1960,　　　in the　Go ld　　Cadillac
Which Is The World　　with　　Go d　　up front
quiet　　with　grandma's earrings and　　gun and
cleaning gloves and bipolar:　　　　　it's　　the
Amy who raised me,　　crying　live　　in　　the
backseat with her hit single　　　'I　Love　You
Let Me Out' for an audience　　of　no　　one:

Live　　　　　in　　Our　　Kitchen
On A Wednesday　　with　　white　　wine
up front (each bottle:　a　　　　　gold
Cadillac (with　a　　little　girl　locked　inside:
it's the Amy I love　　drinking　herself　　live
out of the backseat　　for　an　audience　of
her kids, drowned　　out　by　　　Amy
Winehouse, spilling　　out　of　　the radio:

　　　I can't yell over you, Amy.
　　　It's an old hit:

　　　the song I sing when I
　　　try.

0.

Amy,   I   hate   to   bother
you. But   I   have   to   borrow
your mouth. Sorry.   You   aren't   even
here, but   you're   all   my   Amy
hears. I have to   speak   Winehouse   to
her. Have to have   your   voice,   accent,
the whole thing:

Amy,   your lips   and   lipstick.   I   have   to
put it on   just to   wipe   it   off   again   (like
sobriety (like you on   this page   (like
this page   is   a   kitchen   floor   in
London   wearing you   like   an
earring. I'm so sorry.   I know: you're no
accessory. But   the wine   says:
you are. (Look how   it wears you   like
it is you:

Amy,   you ' r e   i n   e v e r y o n e ' s
mouth   like   gold   teeth   blood   in   Whitney
Houston's   cheek gossip   rag chardonnay easy
imagery   dirty   dishes   whatever   keeps   us
loaded. Like   if we drink   like you,   we'll   be
you.   Like   if the wine   wears us,   we don't
have to. Like   we'll   sing   louder   if   we're
dead.   Like   we   don't have   to   talk   about
it: this disease,   this wanting
to die.   You're in   our   mouth. You   sing
for us: our song,   about going away for
good.   It goes:

            'I can quit anytime I want.   I can quit
            anytime

            I want'
            It's an old hit.

0.

Amy, when   I'm   hungover
and hate myself,   I put on your record
and tattoos and cat eyeliner and   I do
the dishes.   A hundred wine glasses.   Hold
each like   a mic stomach pump halo glass
liver glass head and I wash your hair. I   out-
line the wet lip   of the glass like
it's a new mouth for us all   (I can make it sing
Rehab   An old hit.   Known it since
I was a kid.   It goes:

          'If I hold you here and give
          you water,

          you will   get clean.'
          I'm sorry, it's hard.

1.
Amy, it's ten years today since my sister put you on
the record player and tried to drink herself dead. Four years since

you did it for her. Addiction is a quiet mouth and it doesn't care who
it swallows. You

grabbed your Tanqueray and went back to
Black. Into it, like

it was a vocal booth, a gold Cadillac. Marigolds on, beehive up:
you walked   in humming.

Missy walked   out sober.
Thank you, thank you. She's alive

today and engaged to another fan of yours
Miss Winehouse,

will you go to the wedding with me?
Amy,

                in the reception   in my dreams,   you are sober,
                Mom.

                You turn the wine back   to water because you are
                Great I Love You, live:

                we're dancing, around a dishwasher. We   open
                it and remove   each other live:

                halos spotted, livers clean, we raise
                them like glasses and toast live:

                Loudly, I sing this song for you. It goes:
                'I'm glad you're my mom and a live':

                It's Amy Winehouse & The Water & The Water
                & The Water & My Mom & Sister All Clean

                &
                Alive.

LA FAMILLE

(for Mom, humming to The Sound of Music on TV, half-
asleep but still note-for-note with Julie,   & radiant   & true.)

'   at the very beginning,

A very good place,
    you read
    you sing   with   Me

The first   notes just happen
Do, Re   Do

      I

    name   myself
  a long long
        thread

,

Me,   I call myself
  a long long
   needle
, a note

  will bring us back to

      us   .

  children
Are only
      notes in your head'

You can sing   them up
Like this '

  La Fa Me

    all together

La Fa Me

Good

So we

                             sing

Together
                            sing
                anything

            gold
 ,

            a long long
note

that will bring us back

            La
       Fa
    Me

      you   sing

Me,
   a long long way
         back to

         Me'

1.

Thank you, for being— one of the greatest— um, rock— I mean, uh, a living legend. And um— just, thanks for being on the show.

—Chris Farley
(as Chris Farley

ACTIVATED CHARCOAL HEALING

0.

PROCEDURE: YOUR GOAL IS TO REMOVE
TOXINS   DARK   FLUID   LOOKS
UNAPPETIZING DELIVER IN CORRECT
CONTAINER WHATEVER EASES PATIENT
AND HELPS THEM TO SWALLOW IT WILL
BIND TO POISON IN BODY AND CARRY IT
OUT EXPLAIN YOU HAVE IT ALL OK?   OK:

1.

you laugh and lift a charcoal mask up to my face and
explain how birds' wings get waterlogged and how
we have oil and dirt in our cheeks too but this here
will lift it   out and how it doesn't always work but
the gesture is worth it   and you too have been to
one too many friend funerals and how this helps your
face feel like a face and not a fucking veil   this little
ritual   of lifting   and carrying   out and how
if you're at a Deathmetal show or haunted house with
your Alive Friends you can walk up to the front and
the lightbulbs and loudness will cling to you gorgeous
like fat and you'll glow like a you-size silver trout
and the night sky will be king cake and you'll be
handsome and bright in your old Deathmetal sweater
like Dean Martin but in a Deathmetal sweater and you
will grow into your depression again like old sleeves
and yes i'll still think you're handsome because the
only way to keep the ugly out is to wear it   the only
way to kill death is to eat it   the only way to get
the hell out is to drink it   the only way to get
good medicine is to be it   the only way out of
the fever is through it   the only way out of this
world is wet and carrying an armful of its poison
out with you   like holy black healing water ok lean
back in this   like a dream or bath or best friend
back into the world like an ugly sweater and

1.

yes it is dark but you will glow   yes it is old but
you will be new

119

SYL

(or, What I Should Have Said To My 2002 High School Depression)

0.

hey Hatebreeder,   hey Kappa Khaki Cokehead,   hey DUI Face,
i hate you. and your boatshoes. and imported fists. quit hitting me in the gut.
quit reaching into me like a trust fund. no, i don't have a trust fund. or a ton of
friends.   i have something different:

> (i have an extra-large black magic sweater
> and its name is Deathmetal and it loves me

((yeah, i'm 14.
but my anger is pure and true and shark-shaped.
i listen to Children of Bodom.
they're from *Finland*.
yeah,
you probably haven't heard of them,
but they play Deathmetal and live in my sweater full-time

(((hey hey i have a Deathmetal sweater and
holy crap it's fulla magic.
fat,
and magic.
yeah i know, i'm fat
(and stealthy.
my hands are hidden in my sweater
in crazy pagan formations,
ancient stuff
(haha,
you'll see.

(my hands are small but they're holding crystals.
i have,
like,
a lot of crystals.
gems.
weird stuff.
from Norway.
you don't even know.

((((i do black magic literally all the time (arms on the inside. outside, i'm quiet. yeah, it's because i'm putting a hex on you. it goes: 'aw, bless your bleached heart. i'm gonna put you in my magic sweater. turn you into lyrics.' everything in my sweater is lyrics. it is lyrics. and Deathmetal. everything else sucks.   you suck.   my sweater will eat you.   whatever.

(((((i put your handle of vodka in there. i put your car keys failed breathalyzers expensive yellow polos cigars and thin frat heart in there too. my sweater is ten years sober. i love my sweater. screw you. don't you ever hogtie and choke me in the school closet again, or i'll kill your Escalade. with a nine iron (ok so this has nothing to do with my sweater. i just hate you. with that hot, special hate only a fat kid in August in Houston can conjure. i wear my sweater in ninety degree weather and i'm a young sun and i sweat you out of my bowl cut. i sweat the belly bruises you give me. out of my hands. i write them in your yearbook, into lyrics, just for you:
'g o   t o   h e l l'

((((((hey hey, hey hey hey. heeey, cheer up.   i love you.

(just kidding, i hate you   (what?   (i can't hear you in here. my sweater's listening to Necrophagist. heart like a blast beat. nice 401k. my sweater is grade-a darkness. it takes you in like taxes. thanks, you are living proof that death metal is right: the world out there doesn't want me in it alive   (but this one does

(((((((ok we're writing a new hex. it's not enough to kill you. but you're gonna hate it   (and i hope ya do   (and you have to have it all ok?   (o k a y !:

((((((((my Deathmetal sweater's gonna yawn.
and hug you. all of you.
you'll look little and dapper underneath it,
fallin' on ya like a Sunn O))) show
(like a roof of black noise over the crowd of only you
(like the only thing left will be the big 0
of where you used to go hahaha
((you'll disappear into it like cheap vodka into you like me into your bloody hands like your heart between my teeth like you and i into Catholic school and then this horrible world like this world into the gracious arms of Deathmetal. you'll call out from underneath, begging for reprieve from my hex and i will answer:

'h   m   m   m

yeah ok,
but first can i finish this chocolate cake?'

(you will take a backseat to my chocolate cake.   and wait   and learn
and believe   in the Deathmetal around you, and the chubby 14–year old who
alone is worthy to wield it. who is pure of heart and trve, with a healthy hate and
laundry list of heroes with broke heads and hearts and hands and big mouths:

0.
Devin Townsend tailored his bipolar into a band. Cattle Decapitation
has written two decades of obscene songs for animal rights. Lord
Worm howled on 'None So Vile' when he wasn't teaching English.
John of the Cross wrote poems in a church prison with no light. The
Virgin Mary ascended to heaven in a chariot   (it was a
black sweater

> 0.
> we all have this darkness.
> you can keep it in your blood and become it
>
> (or howl it out, wear it all around, have a
> dip in the hatebath (while the waters warm!
>
> let it gobble you up and yank
> out your bleached teeth on stage
>
> (and i will too
> (bleeding, bawling:
>
> 666.
> 'your house is burning down but good news!:
> you can live inside Deathmetal.
>
> hey asshole, one day you're gonna die but good news!:
> my Deathmetal sweater will live on and on and on
>
> in glory and hate eternal,
> without you.'

ACTIVATED DIY BLACK METAL HEALING RITUAL

1.
'hey buddy, question: do y'all still carry activated charcoal
on your trucks? is it still the go-to intervention for OD?'

1.
'AUSTIN DIDN'T. OAK HILL DIDN'T.
WE DON'T HAVE IT IN OUR BAGS IN SA. I'M
NOT SURE ABOUT THE AMBULANCES
THOUGH   EVERYONE IS PHASING IT
OUT SINCE IT'S MORE TROUBLE THAN
IT'S WORTH UNLESS YOU KNOW WHAT
EXACTLY   THEY   SWALLOWED   YOU
MIGHT NOT WANT IT COMING BACK
UP   A FEW INSTRUCTORS SAY IT JUST
MAKES A BIG FUCKING MESS HAH LIKE WE
HAD   A   GUY WHO HAD   JUST
SWALLOWED A BOTTLE OF SOME KIND OF
PAIN KILLER   HIS MOM CALLED IT IN   NO
SIGNS WHEN WE GOT THERE BUT WE JUST
QUICKLY PACKAGED HIM   THE MEDICS
JUST SAID THEY WERE GONNA START AN I
V HAVE NARCAN READY   AND MONITOR
HIM ON THE WAY TO   THE HOSPITAL'

1.
'oh i see.
ok thanks.'

0.
(i'm afraid this wont even have a tiny kvlt
following   ((i'm afraid i won't ever help anyone

PAW

0.

yeah huh my grandpa says	hey- hey-
hey my Pawpaw says:	when god spoke
us into existence, he	slurred and forgot his
words.	

wanted to say 'bright' but said 'bone' and here
we are with such darkness in us. wanted to
say 'crown' but it came out 'chemo' and lord
we hate our hair. he said 'want' instead of 'wind'
and now we hold our breath and say 'I' and point to
this body (this luggage

0.

hey, hey if you say 'Bloody Mary' into the mirror five
times fast, your lil' sis will appear before you and talk.
yeah huh,   yeah i did it and she told me:

'No, Booboo. This ain't blood, it's cooking oil.
Heaven tastes like eggs. I am bloated on it. I, like you,
have unhinged my jaw to take in all of this feeling (
but you are not what you eat. You are not your
sadness (that's your body talking. Your body talks like
Pawpaw and says 'mais i got the pawdes, mon chra. i
got the paw.' It's a Cajun family dish: this grogginess,
this tired-of-living. 'Sad' is a lie your stupid body tells
you (so take off

your body) Stuff it down the sink. Clog the toilet with
your dumb bones. When the plate of this world has
been licked clean and you're sleepysick, repeat this
recipe: '

0.

hey if you say 'Grandpa' five times fast your veins will
fill   with   bayou   and   you'll   die   and   leap
out your own goddamn body like catfish)

hey if you say 'Grandma' five times fast, you'll wake

124

up like a baby snake and bite your way out
your body)

hey if you say 'Louisiana' five times fast, sure enough,
your little eyes will become eggs. Everything will look
cracking and born at the same bloody time)

hey if you say 'Summertime' once under your breath
you'll see your dead best friend in the hallway. You
won't know why he's yelling)

hey if you say 'I Love You' to anyone ever again, on
cue, your ex will walk out the closet like fog, like hot
breath, and sit on the bed with y'all. They won't
actually be there, but will fall on you anyways like a
quilt with their whole mouth)

hey if you say 'Mikey' you'll leave the world. If you say
'Christopher' you'll leave the world. If you say
'William', 'Happy', '4th of July', 'Houston', or
anything at all, you will eventually die) so why not say
everything)

hey if some sad god spoke you into that sad body, ya
know you can)   speak yourself)   out of it)
yeah huh yeah   watch:

1.

creosote)   mouthwash)   boudain bill)
bourré bill)   oh lovely Lorraine)   oh chocolate-
covered strawberries)   oh chocolate-covered
heart)   oh chocolate-hearted Christ and rifle kisser)
how loud our sweet shells do crack)   Aunt Lily)
Aunt Lily) butterfly knife) wife) casino) mom and dad)

1.

i got words in my cheeks like cotton)   i   d
o the genesis dance   snakes and all
a   b   r   a   c   a   d   a   b   r   a   :
i create as i speak   i utter everything   i utter myself
into the world. my mouth is an airboat and god is the
air)   i   dive

into your bayou,   l o r d   i s w i m
in you and   i forget that long weekend i watched
my Momo   die (at the mouth of the river,
i recall: my grandpa played my blue guitar for
three   whole   days   'til he   fell   out   his
body) Marymoo, watch: i'm gonna kill   my
body)   and live   in   that   blue
guitar instead   and shine   and shed
my skin)   and sing   all the right
words

1.
Oh yeah well if god spoke us into existence, then my
grandpa did the same thing to god with that guitar.
god was asleep but Pawpaw woke Him up. Saw Him
in Himself in that mirror and hooked Him with a
guitar neck, and yanked God

                                    out)

                        by the cheek like

                            a catfish

                        that was sick of

                            the water

                        and living:

1.

'I'm dying'
'Is it blissful?'

'It's like a dream.'
'I want to dream.'

—Deafheaven

GLORY TO GOD FOR LONGSLEEVES

((ok my arms are wings and i cut mouths into
my wings into the here heavy and they chant: i go up
and up. and then i go up and up. and one day i go up
and up and up and don't go back down. but one time
i went up and up and then i went up and but one day
i'll open up and up i'll up and up uh huh i'll went up
and up into the sky and i won't will come back down.
yeah i go go up and up up. and then yes, one day i,
yes, i am will go up and and up. and then one day i
giveup yeah go away and giveup and up n up n up n
up. and i want to give up and go away. but i wanna
give up wannawanna yeah go away up and up and up
and up into heaven. i wanna be god's fist. i wanna up
and up. i wanna be reach and reach up and up and up.
i wanna open godfist. i want a hungover god to
drink me up and up and up from the griefwater
iwanna go up and up, on the up and up. i go up and
up always up and up. but then, yeah, but i wanna yeah
i wanna go up and up and up and up. one day i go up
and up and up and up and upand don't go back
down. no i wanna don't wanna wanna die up and aup
up up and up and up in the hot hot sky and then up
and up and higher i up and up higher and higher up
and up and up and up and up and upa nadup and up
and i gonna give up and up and go away up and oh
no oh no i cut my arm up and up on the bathroom
floor i made a messup and up i'm so sunk lord i have
to teach today how will i teach english class now but
hosanna hosanna,   the tv weatherman announces
a quick chill,   a kindness:

holy, holy: this unexpected

wind: this cold front:

these long   sleeves:

                                              ))

131

HEIR LOOM

0.

ok watch: i'm in Galveston or the Gold Coast or anywhere and a guy gropes me on the train and then i hate my fat and not-wings and want to die all over again so i go to the movies   (ok i sit in a dark room in a dark chair and watch giant beautiful humans laughing in the air above me and i love them and leave my seat and float up and disappear (i n t o the screen:

(ok a pelican is in the living room   he   opens
his wings   (ok   watch:

(on the screen   a   pelican
is wearing pearls   he   opens
his wings like wet cheeks (keep watching:

(on the screen, there's either   a   pelican
or my lonely grandpa. i eat   p o p c o r n
or pills out of his mouth   (c a p t i o n s :

(look at this bird: little and gold. his name
is bipolar and he's an   heirloom and he's yours
ok?   (look how handsome:

(and then i'm on the screen in a bathtub with pearl bracelets and broken hands and then i open my wings   (

and then i open my wings   (

and then i open   (my wings and wings
and wrists and words and wow   (l o
o k how big i am haha everyone have a good look:

(now i'm on the screen and i'm in every seat and i'm on the screen but i'm also on the screen and i am the whole screen too and i look right at the camera and say:

(quit looking at me   like i'm alive and
here. i hate that   (look: i'm not really human
(i'm only a movie and i have   a script ok? it's called
I Love You But I'm Leaving   it's easy and quiet and
ends early before anyone   i love gets sad walks
out first   (oh   it   lets   everyone
down it sells out every night   i buy all the tickets
i've seen it a hundred times and i hate it but i have to
watch: oh ok lo   ok: the   popcorn
tears and depression in diva lights and the audio
cuts and the captions over my face:

(fuck this film of my head   and how easy it
imagines me dead   and that dead kid
who's supposed to be the adult me   look: i   look
too handsome i when i die   i don't buy it, william
fuck your forearms   they aren't wings or
film reels   they're   forearms,
heirlooms   fuck you for opening
them on film in front of us   (it doesn't look fake
(all your friends are afraid all your good lines will be
(cut (cut   (i look right at the camera:

i love you but i'm leaving (cut   i love you but i (cut
i love leaving (cut   i   love   i (cut
i'm love le (cut   i   love you (but
i love you but i love you but   i love you i love you
i love you and i'm writing   a   better   script:

an ugly movie with ugly birds) buckshot) beads) humans who hate themselves but love each other) who end too early but are here long as they can be) it'll go too long) it'll hang from our eyes like pearls) and i wear it) and walk out of the ugly bill of the   screen)   wet   and   bright   and
new   ok
open   on:

1.

The Gold Coast)

A lot of palm trees)

A train going through it)

All the rain)

1000 pelican eyes)

up in the Australian night)

I see it)

I see it)

and I say the only line I have:)

I am glad I didn't kill myself before I saw this.

1.
And that's it: the end. Lights, credits
thank you to everyone I love in every seat, still
watching out for me. I eat your applause like
popcorn. I wear it like pearls. I am a new
movie. It's called Everyone I Love and it opens on:
us like a necklace. Oh, oh
you have to watch it ok? Ok here:
watch, watch:

1.

Time to wake up.

—Yob

I AM BECAUSE YOU ARE   /   I WILL BE BECAUSE YOU WERE

1.

ACTIVATED CHARCOAL: YOUR GOAL IS TO REMOVE   TOXIN   FROM   SYSTEM ADMINISTER   MED   AND   TRANSPORT REPORT NAME DOSE ROUTE TIME AND CHANGE IN MENTAL STATUS   REASSESS INTERVENTIONS   DOCUMENT IT ALL MANY WILL VOMIT AND WON'T BE ABLE TO FINISH ENCOURAGE THEM   EXPLAIN YOU HAVE TO HAVE IT ALL   OK TRY HARD NOT TO GIVE UP OR VOMIT OK? OK HERE YOU GO: OK   HERE:

1.

' I'm so happy you're here. Thank you for making it out tonight.   I   know   you've   been   going through hell.   It's ok,   ok?   I went through it too.   In '88, right before we were blessed with you,   I checked into that haunted house. Dante without a Virgil. Three weeks in, I was sick of burnt hospital food and oh God about to give up for good   (And then I had you

1.

And then I had you
then I had you
I had you
I had you
I had you
I had you
with me. I had you
walking. I had you
wading. I had you
I add you
you
you
you
u

)

'with me and thank God I did because I walked
out of hell and ended up here. With you.
At your sister's rehearsal dinner.   Eating
too much of this bread. I   had   you
in my dreams. Your chubby arms
r e a c h i n g up   and   up,
o p e n i n g your   fists   like
spoons of cough syrup. M e d i c i n e .
You're sick right now but you are medicine. O my
handsome kid, even at your ugliest, we love the hell
out of you. And if you have to disappear again, and fall
back   into   it,   it's   ok.   Ok?   You   know
that   you'll   always   have   a   home   to
come back to. All of us are waiting in the kitchen.
We have a gumbo on. Ok. Thank you for coming
home tonight. And being with us. I mean, alive. And

here:

ACTIVATED DOWN & OUT HEALING

1.

ok i understand.
thank you, i love you.

i am going through it again
(the instructions:

1.

It says in 18th century Ireland, 'sin eaters' were hired to eat bread off of the chests of the recently deceased, absorbing the sins that have soaked into it, helping dead loved ones into Heaven

It says Dante and Virgil, weary and frightened, climbed up the Devil's back to get out of Hell

It says lungfish are able to breathe both in and out of water

1.

i hate myself so often it's like breathing. sorry. i wish i wasn't so hungry. Hell's hard to stomach but (thanks to a great great great Irish grandpa) i have a big mouth. we do our best with what we're given.

yes i still want to die most days but i don't think that's a good or bad thing. it's just a thing, that we go into: inferno haunted house blanket fort Deathmetal oven ugly water anything we can sit inside of and talk with old friends again   and a g a i n
into it   and b a c k
out again   here:

1.

One day I'll be 80 and depressed and I'll want to die all over again and then I won't. Again. I'll still be

here:

1.
This morning, on the floor with you. Here, my chest is an oven. Here, I'm sitting my computer on top. Here, this book rises up from the keys. Here, I baked you this bread. It's a lot but here, I'll help you clean your plate. Here, let's eat this page like gauze. Here:

1.
It says everything we eat is processed sunshine. So here:

this morning   Here, this light   Here,   coffee
Here this hangover cure   Here   eucharist
buffet   Here   the   horror   movie   and
hymnal   the haunted house and chapel   and
xanax and champagne and the salt and salt   and
the bathroom tile and ambulance floor   the wedding
cake and funeral food   dandelions and Bourbon street
bloody lip and wineglass   the   blue   blazer   and
black sweater   king cake in best friend's hand
beignet in sister's mouth   water   in   the   wineglass
the gold Cadillac and tree sap   catfish and bright hook
and Deathmetal and ugly medicine and old blood and
new gauze and 0 and 1   you and i   you and i:

sunshine   each word, a hand dipped in light
like we are   oily birds eating out of our own bills
lapping up   the   dark   like   cough   syrup
taking the haunted house   with us,   in pieces
eyes yawning   open,   we   are
hickeys on   the   necks   of
God and the Devil   climbing   ,
kissing   this   paper   hard   ,
it has mourning breath.   it says: there's   no   way
out   (and   that's   the   way
out.   you   can
carry your darkness   with   you
(into   the   light:

down,   down,

and out   here:

1.

It's nice outside.

I've soaked up death
like gauze, like bread. But

the air today is clean,
whether or not

I am too.
I hope

the bread in Heaven is good.
I hope

I'll have it with you one day,
but not today.

It's ok.
It'll be ok.

(I'm going
outside now,

ok?
Ok.

I'm going
out:

WORKS CITED
(in order of appearance)

Much of the language from "Healing Ritual" poems comes straight from old EMS class/field notes, originally transcribed from *Emergency Transportation for the Sick and Injured*, 9th edition (Jones & Bartlett, 2005).

"The Chris Farley Show: Paul McCartney." *Saturday Night Live* (Season 18 Episode 13). NBC, 13 Feb 1993.

Dead Kennedys. "California Über Alles." *Fresh Fruit for Rotting Vegetables*, Alternative Tentacles, 1980.

Converge. "All We Love We Leave Behind." *All We Love We Leave Behind*, Deathwish Inc, 2012.

Oathbreaker. "Needles In Your Skin." *Rheia*, Deathwish Inc, 2016.

Dante quotes and references from BBC Radio 4's broadcast of *The Inferno* (2014), and an audiobook of *The Inferno*, translated by Robert Pinsky (Recorded Books, 2013).

Cephalic Carnage. "Dying Will Be the Death of Me." *Anomalies*, Relapse Records, 2005.

Sikth. *Death of a Dead Day*, Bieler Bros Records, 2006.

Gojira. "The Art of Dying." *The Way of All Flesh*, Listenable Records, 2008.

Cryptopsy. "The Frantic Pace of Dying.". *Once Was Not*,

Century Media Records, 2005.

Cryptopsy. "Dead and Dripping." *None So Vile*, Wrong
    Again Records, 1996.

At The Gates. "Into the Dead Sky." *Slaughter of the Soul*,
    Earache Records, 1995.

Opeth. "Serenity Painted Death." *Still Life*, Peaceville Records, 1999.

Bloodbath. "Breeding Death." *Breeding Death*, Century
    Media Records, 2000.

Dimmu Borgir. *Death Cult Armageddon*, Nuclear Blast,
    2003.

"Texas is the reason that the president's dead" is a reference to "Bullet"
    by *The Misfits* (Static Age, Caroline Records, 1996).

Hearne, Vicki. "Can An Ape Tell A Joke? Learning From
    A Las Vegas Orangutan Act." *Harper's Magazine*,
    1993.

Cult Leader. "Lightless Walk." *Lightless Walk*, Deathwish
    Inc, 2015.

"Simia Dei" is from Giorgio Agamben's *The Open: Man
    and Animal* (Stanford University Press, 2004) and
    Old Man Gloom's "Simia Dei" (*The Ape of God*,
    Profound Lore, 2014).

Bellylaugh inspired by an entry in *Around the Year with Emmett Fox*
    (Harper Collins, 2009).

Tommy Boy. Dir. Peter Segal. Perf. Chris Farley and David Spade.

Paramount Pictures, 1995.

"Matt Foley: Talking to Kids About Drugs." *Saturday Night Live* (Season 18 Episode 19). NBC, 8 May 1993.

Shakespeare, William, J. J. M. Tobin, and G. Blakemore Evans. "The Riverside Shakespeare." Houghton Mifflin, 1997.

Altar of Plagues. "Reflection Pulse Remains." *Teethed Glory & Injury*, Profound Lore Records, 2013.

The Stitches. "My Baby Hates Me." *8x12*, Vinyl Dog Records, 1995.

Thou (from "Drowning Injury Healing Ritual") is an excellent doom metal band from Baton Rouge. Go visit their record shop, Sisters in Christ (5206 Magazine St, New Orleans, LA.)

Mgła. "Exercises In Futility VI." *Exercises In Futility*, No Solace, 2015.

Zao. "Physician, Heal Thyself." *The Fear Is What Keeps Us Here*, Ferret Music, 2006.

Epigraph in "Walt Disney's New Camera" is from the "Tricks of our Trade" Disney video short (Disneyland, 1957).

Isis. "Hym" and "The Beginning and the End." *Oceanic*, Ipecac Recordings, 2002.

"The Good Times Are Killing Me" was written on the accordion case of Cajun music legend Nathan Abshire, and is also the title of his record with the Balfa Brothers (Swallow Records, 1975).

Amy Winehouse. "Rehab" and "You Know I'm No
	Good." *Back to Black*, Island Records, 2006.

"La Famille" is an erasure of the lyrics to "Do–Re–Mi"
	from the musical *Sound of Music* starring Julie Andrews
	(Richard Rodgers and Oscar Hammerstein II, 1959)

"SYL" is a popular acronym for Canadian metal legends
	Strapping Young Lad.

"Hatebreeder" is the title of Children of Bodom's second album.

Second stanza of "Activated DIY Black Metal Healing
	Ritual" is a text message from poet/musician/fire
	fighter/EMT/punk/Die-Hard enthusiast and best-
	friend Kevin Winchester "Velocirapstar" Burke.

Deafheaven. "Dream House." *Sunbather*, Deathwish Inc, 2013.

Yob. "In Our Blood." *Clearing the Path* to Ascend, Neurot Recordings,
	2014.

THANK YOU

1.

To   Kim & Blue Weber   Mom & Dad   Missy and Mary Moran   Dillon Murski   Laura Mullen   Sue Weinstein   Chris Barrett   Randolph Thomas   Adam Davy   Simon Kindt   Scott Wings   Brady Ware   Phil Griffin   Kevin W Burke   The Bordelon Gauthier and Jeansonne families   Hanif Willis-Abdurraqib   sam sax   William James   William Brian Sain   Madison Mae Parker   Lino Anunciacion   Gary Lovely   Justin Greene   Derrick Brown   The couple of patients and partners who told me I was doing a good job when they didn't have to   The artists who have howled with and for me   The shows I've laid inside of instead of on a stretcher   Everyone who saw me at my lowest and didn't look away   Who sat with me on the tile   Who thought my ugly howling was worth hearing   Who drank my noise like medicine and made me have half   Who held my cup   To God who lets me dress and nickname him a hundred different ways   To You You You, still reading   You, still here in whatever way you can be   You, who stayed as long as you could   To Christopher Crosby Farley   To Tabitha from the crisis center who was very kind on the phone   And most of all   To Michael Patrick Siebenthal   Who was a true friend when no one else was   i am because you are   i will be because you were

1.

Additional thanks to the following journals for giving these odd little numbers a home (in current or previous form), or for their general support:

-*Bird's Thumb*: "Bildungsroman ((a guided tour"
-*Pressure Gauge Press*: "I'm walking through a haunted house in Louisiana and won't keep my big mouth shut", "RTSD", "give up yeah go away", "Godsalt", and "i am trying"
-*Drunk in a Midnight Choir*: "An Usher Has Questions", "The Cement Whispers To Dustin", and "I Don't Want to Want to Die"

–*Phoebe*: "Paw"

–*LUX*: "bowie knife"

–*Button Poetry* (video): "Bildungsroman ((a guided tour", "Paw",
        "King Cake"

–*Write About Now Poetry* (video): "Paw", "Heir Loom", "O.S.R."

–*Melbourne Spoken Word* (video and audio): "Godsalt"

–*Timbermouse*

–*Alien Mouth*

ABOUT THE AUTHOR

Bill Moran is a third-year MFA poetry candidate at Louisiana State University and a former medic. He was the 2012 & 2013 Austin Poetry Slam Champion; has performed and taught poetry throughout the US, Australia, and Southeast Asia; and served as president of Mic Check, a non-profit poetry organization in Brazos County, Texas. His work has appeared or is forthcoming in Button Poetry (video), Phoebe, Bird's Thumb, Next Left Press, FreezeRay Press, LUX, Alien Mouth, Pressure Gauge Press, and Drunk in a Midnight Choir. He co-authored his first book of poetry, *Wreck / Age*, with Simon Kindt and it is available now through Alien Mouth. He appreciates your concern and well-wishes, but swears he is okay. Really.

www.billmoranpoetry.com

Author Photo: Christopher Diaz

If you like Bill Moran, Bill likes...

Drunks and Other Poems of Recovery
Jack McCarthy

Amulet
Jason Bayani

Over the Anvil We Stretch
Anis Mojgani

This Way to the Sugar
Hieu Minh Nguyen

Write Bloody Publishing distributes and promotes great books of poetry every year. We are an independent press dedicated to quality literature and book design.

Our employees are authors and artists so we call ourselves a family. Our design team comes from all over America: modern painters, photographers and rock album designers create book covers we're proud to be judged by.

We have published over 115 titles to date. We are grass-roots, D.I.Y., bootstrap believers. Pull up a good book and join the family. Support independent authors, artists and presses.

WRITEBLOODY
QUALITY AMERICAN BOOKS

Want to know more about Write Bloody books, authors and events?
Join our maling list at

www.writebloody.com

WRITE BLOODY BOOKS

CPSIA information can be obtained
at www.ICGtesting.com
Printed in the USA
FSOW02n0446280317
32302FS

9 781938 912689